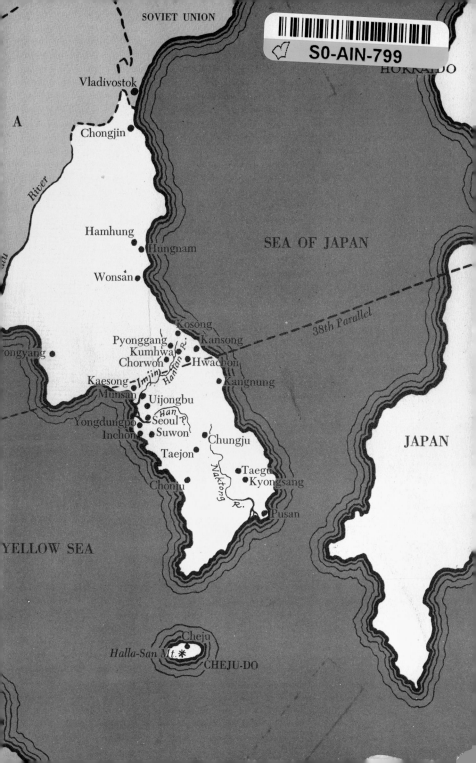

SOVIET UNION

HOKKAIDO

S0-AIN-799

Vladivostok

A

Chongjin

River

SEA OF JAPAN

Hamhung

Hungnam

Wonsan

38th Parallel

Kosong

Pyonggang

Kansong

Kumhwa

Chorwon

Hwacheon

ongyang

Kaesong

Imjin

Hantan R.

Kangnung

Munsan

Uijongbu

Han

JAPAN

Yongdungpo

Seoul

Inchon

Suwon

Chungju

Taejon

Naktong

Taegu

Kyongsang

Chonju

R.

Pusan

YELLOW SEA

Cheju

Halla-San Mt.

CHEJU-DO

The
Peculiar War

Impressions
of a
Reporter
in Korea

The

Peculiar War

Impressions of a

Reporter in Korea

by E. J. Kahn, Jr.

Random House • New York

Except for Chapters 9 and 11,
the material in this book
originally appeared, some of it in slightly
different form, in *The New Yorker*, to which
acknowledgment is gratefully made.

First Printing

Copyright, 1951, 1952, by E. J. Kahn, Jr.

Published in New York by Random House, Inc., and
simultaneously in Toronto, Canada, by Random
House of Canada, Limited

Library of Congress Catalog Card Number: 52-5554

Manufactured in the United States of America
By The Haddon Craftsmen, Inc., Scranton, Pa.

Designer: Ernst Reichl

For Terry and Joey,
who've never had to ride pick-a-back,
thank God, except for the fun of it.

Preface

I SPENT nearly three months in Korea as a correspondent for *The New Yorker,* arriving early in April,
1951, a few days before General MacArthur was relieved, and departing late in June, a few days before
the cease-fire negotiations began. This book is in no
sense supposed to be a complete account of the war
in Korea, for, of course, I was not present during a
great deal of it—the retreat of the United Nations
troops toward the south after the North Koreans
started it all, the first swing back of the pendulum
and the ensuing advance to the Yalu River, the hasty
flight from there when the Chinese entered the pic-

ture, and the subsequent reorganization of the Eighth Army, under General Ridgway, from a fairly demoralized outfit into a cocky and competent fighting force. Nor, indeed, is this book a complete account even of that phase of the war I was privileged to witness. It is, rather, a report on some of the things I saw and heard while there that interested me, and that I thought people at home might not otherwise know about and might be interested in, too. To many, the Korean War seems to have been incomprehensible; perhaps these pages will make aspects of it, at least, more understandable to some.

I was an extremely lucky correspondent. For one thing, I missed both the intense cold of the winter and the intense heat of the summer, and thus got to know only at second hand about some of the most formidable discomforts that have attended an exceptionally uncomfortable war. I was also lucky because, not having to file dispatches about the day-to-day changes in the tactical situation, I was free to wander around pretty much wherever I wanted to, and write whatever I wanted to. From the point of view of practically anybody else who has recently traveled to the troubled peninsula once known as the Land of the Morning Calm, I was luckiest of all, undoubtedly, in that after what by local standards was a relatively brief stay there, I was able to leave the place and go home.

E. J. K.

Scarborough, N. Y., October, 1951

The
Peculiar War

*Impressions
of a
Reporter
in Korea*

1

ALMOST at the very moment that the news of General MacArthur's relief was coming over the radio at the divisional command post on the western front where I was staying on that eventful April 11th, a terrific wind blew across the camp site, leveling a couple of tents. A few minutes later, a hailstorm lashed the countryside, forcing jeep drivers—who had not long before been ordered to take the tops off their vehicles in deference to the belief, then prevailing more strongly than ever, that the Chinese were about to throw their air force into the war—to pull up. A few hours after that, there was a driving snowstorm.

3

Since the weather had been fairly springlike for the previous couple of weeks, the odd climatic goings on prompted one soldier—who, like the majority of the men in the United Nations forces, habitually, if not always reverently, referred to MacArthur in terms usually reserved for the Deity—to exclaim, "Gee, do you suppose he really is God, after all?"

A couple of days earlier, a regimental commander, asked how one of his battalions was making out a couple of miles away from his command post, said he thought it was doing all right but couldn't be sure. "The farther back you are, of course, the less you know," he said. Politically speaking, front-line soldiers are usually very much in the rear echelon, and in the first few hours after the change in command their ignorance of what had been going on in Washington and Tokyo was immense. (It quickly became known, however, that some of the British troops serving in the polyglot Eighth Army threw quite a party the night the news broke.) General Ridgway, at a press conference he held at an advance Eighth Army headquarters shortly before he acquired his new portfolio of titles, gave no hint—if, indeed, he had received any himself—of the tremendous upheaval that was about to occur. He did say, in the course of announcing the impending arrival in Korea

4

of Secretary of the Army Pace, that Mr. Pace had a fine sense of humor, but it was probably merely coincidence that the man he thus characterized happened to be, at the moment of the revelation of MacArthur's dethronement, standing almost exactly astride the Thirty-eighth Parallel, tugging on a lanyard to launch a shell from a 155-mm. rifle, which, of all the big guns used in Korea, makes the biggest and most earth-shaking bang.

In mid-April, actually, the soldiers fighting in Korea were much less concerned with the possibility that the eleventh of that month might become historic than with the imminence of May 1st, which, being a significant date for the Communists, was regarded as a likely time for the detonation of some especially explosive Chinese fireworks. On the eleventh, one rifle-company sergeant, hitchhiking his way back from the front to a battalion aid station, climbed aboard a jeep and, when asked what he thought about the day's big news, said, "Oh, yeah. I hear Mac got fired," and let it go at that. It was a statement of simple, and remote, fact.

At the time the team of Ridgway and Van Fleet was substituted for that of MacArthur and Ridgway, undoubtedly the most unexpected change in a high-powered lineup since Jim Konstanty started the first game of the 1950 World Series, the United Nations forces were patiently continuing the slow, difficult northward progress they had been making in what Ridgway frequently described as "a war of maneuver." Most of the actions of the early spring had been exceptionally modest in scale, though not invariably so reported. One version of a joke then being circulated in Korea had a soldier saying, "I was attacked by two hordes and killed both of them"; a variation had him asking, "How many hordes to a platoon?" To those officers occupied with the big picture, if not the very big, international picture, the presence to their immediate north of Communist forces in large numbers, with their air potential and it was anybody's guess what else, was no joke at all, but at the regimental level and forward it is always hard not to be much less preoccupied with such matters than with what may be sitting on the next couple of hills ahead. For instance, the fact that four American Rangers were unaccounted for on one tiny segment of the front and the fact that a Turkish company commander had been killed a bit to their left were just as big topics of conversation among the soldiers on the western front on the eleventh of April as the fantastic news trickling in over the radio. To be sure, the casualties then being suffered by our forces were relatively light, a state of affairs that was to change considerably in a fortnight, but that did not make them any the less important. Passing a spot where the dead from one American regiment were being collected, a division staff officer, who had been talking about the assault of a particular hill, glanced at a jeep on which lay a litter bearing a single shrouded corpse. "You never get it for free," he said.

By mid-April, much of the Korean battleground was thoroughly familiar to the United Nations troops, then on the second northward swing of their seesawing trek up and down a peninsula that, no matter how small it may look on a map, used to contain thirty million people and is about equal in size to England and Scotland. Across most of the front, our forces were occupying ground several miles north of the celebrated Parallel, which—except when decorated with heavy artillery batteries or eminent visitors from Washington—is indistinguishable from most of the rest of the terrain. Korea is a land of interminable hills and valleys and streams, with the hills predominating. It is an age-old boast of some of its full-time inhabitants that one cannot step three feet from the threshold of any home in their country without having a mountain in view, and few soldiers who have served there would be inclined to dispute

7

this claim. Many of the hills are crowned with rock cliffs. Even those with softer crests are no cinch to climb, particularly under combat conditions. A few days before I got to Korea, one infantry company, in the course of having to make two round trips up and down a single, average-size hill, had suffered sixteen exhaustion casualties. Newcomers to the region were apt to comment, as I did when I arrived, on its scenic attractiveness—on the lower slopes of some of the hills, for instance, terraced paddies rise up from the valleys, constituting a nice combination of utility and beauty—but after a couple of days it loses its charm. As one drove along the dirt roads, the best of which were built by the Japanese during their administration of the much put-upon country, one's interest in vistas was likely to be quickly supplanted by an interest in bumps. When it rains or hails or snows, the roads turn into mud. When it doesn't rain, the roads become thickly coated with the kind of dust that, once it infiltrates one's lungs, seems never to be altogether extricable. Even the best of the roads were no match for a protracted assault of mechanized traffic. As a result, anybody who had to get some place in a hurry, and had authority enough to command the necessary transportation, traveled by air. Generals inspected their regiments and battalions by light plane, or heli-

8

copter. Since most of the helicopters on hand could accommodate only one person in addition to the pilot, the Korean War was notably tough on generals' aides, who in previous struggles were wont to tag along in their commanders' vehicles. In Korea, while a general cruised serenely above the snarled traffic on the roads, his aide could frequently be found traveling frustratedly, and alone, in a jeep down below, hoping that he could somehow get to wherever the old man was going before the old man fluttered on to some other destination.

The mountains over which the United Nations troops conscientiously plodded—it hadn't taken them long to learn that one good way of forestalling human infiltration was to survey all the land they conquered, leaving no little unexplored patches through which the enemy might seep—were pitted with shell craters and scarred by white phosphorus and napalm, but otherwise ornamented mainly with stunted evergreens and scrub oaks. In the early spring, they were uniformly a bleak brown in color. Then, as if by magic, they were completely and gloriously carpeted with azaleas. Then the azaleas died, and they turned bleak again. There are plenty of flowers in Korea, but they somehow seem to serve only to point up the shabbiness of the place. The first ones I saw there were the blossoms on a cherry tree in Taegu. And it was perhaps symbolic of Korea that the cherry tree was right next to an Army latrine.

Along every road in Korea was a sorrowful and familiar sight—the remains of villages that once consisted of a dozen or more tile- or thatched-roof huts of stone and wood and dirt, but, with exceptions so rare as to be conspicuous, had been razed to the ground, by one or another of the weapons from the devastating arsenal of democracy. Despite the lack of visible shelter left to them, Koreans were still living in these villages, scratching up what means of existence they could. In the paddy fields, farmers could be seen employing a labor-saving device peculiar to the country: the three-man shovel. One man wields the shovel handle. He has two assistants, each of whom helps in the manipulation of the implement by tugging at a rope threaded through a metal ring riveted to either side of the shovel blade. I have no idea whether such collaborative work was prompted by indolence or unemployment. There were other variations on this same theme. In the rear areas, Korean youths often worked in pairs as shoeshine boys, one to a foot; and along river banks, whole platoons of them participated in the washing of a single vehicle.

10

Some Koreans had been attached to our combat units and traveled around with them. One division I stayed with had nearly five thousand in tow, each of whom received a couple of portions of rice daily and was paid the equivalent of about a dollar a week. These Koreans were generally known by the informal designation of the "A-Frame Army." Aside from those residents of the country who are fortunate enough to own an ox and a cart, nearly all the villagers customarily carry whatever they have to carry on their backs. They strap their loads to a wooden contraption that looks like the letter "A," and they can tote staggering burdens with this device—well over a hundred pounds up a steep mountain trail, for instance. The Koreans in the A-Frame Army lugged rations and ammunition up hills, helped the engineers build roads, and dug the graves in which the Communist dead were buried and, not infrequently, in which some of their own dead were, since the native bearers accompanied our most forward units and were subject to the same hazards the soldiers were. (Our own dead were taken care of, as is customary, by Graves Registration teams.) Whenever the Eighth Army moved north of the Thirty-eighth Parallel, many of the civilians who hung around its installations and could freely observe its deployment and equipment were, inevitably, North Koreans, but, the war being a peculiar one, the circumstance that they happened to be enemy aliens didn't seem to make anybody pay special attention to their apparently aimless wanderings—with all their meagre belongings piled high on their extraordinarily strong backs, and the younger children riding pick-a-back, like as not, on the only slightly sturdier shoulders of the older ones—from one scarred village to another.

Just before being elevated to his new and high commands, General Ridgway, then speaking solely as a tactical man, expressed the view that no immediate conclusion to the fighting was foreseeable. The idea that the war, barring some kind of non-battle-field settlement, was an endless one was almost universally accepted by the men involved in it, and this feeling didn't make things easy for the combat troops, particularly since they hadn't anything to take their minds off their formidable work when they were out of the line. At rare—exceedingly rare—intervals, they got five-day furloughs to Japan, a place that to those soldiers who were on Occupation duty there prior to the war had come to mean home, if a second home. (These temporal oases were called "R and R," standing, according to higher authorities, for "Rest and Rehabilitation," and, according to nearly everyone else, for "Rape and Restitution.") The great majority of them, however, had very little to do during their off-duty hours. Money was almost worthless, since there was practically nothing to spend it on. One day, I saw two rifle companies playing an intra-battalion softball game, on a diamond laid out on a paddy field, for a purse of a thousand dollars.

The main subject of conversation among the troops was rotation. In April, the first contingents of veteran soldiers headed back to the United States. They represented only about one per cent of our total strength, but the fact that some men were actually getting out of Korea, presumably for good, had a tonic effect on nearly everybody. When a hillbilly troupe turned up one day and put on a show, the most acclaimed number by far was a non-hillbilly song, clearly of recent origin, entitled "The Rotation Blues." High-ranking officers were just as virulently infected with rotation fever as anyone else, and although enlisted men do not usually take a sympathetic view of the personal gripes of the brass, one brigadier general, who had just arrived at that exalted rank when rotation began, found it possible to cry on any shoulder he cared to. He had gone through eight nasty months of the war before he received his star, but nonetheless he learned a few days after he got it, from a list put out by the

13

Department of the Army, that, according to a regulation that governs the exclusive world of generals, he was credited with zero months of foreign service. The generals at the top of the list were a few of MacArthur's right-hand men, one of whom had not long before completed something like a hundred and fifty-six consecutive months of overseas duty. Nobody knew for sure, as May Day loomed near, just when and where the enemy would strike, but there was little doubt that that list would soon be extensively revised.

2

RIGHT after breakfast one morning in April, I left the command post of the 25th Infantry Division, where I was staying for a while, and about an hour later arrived at a river crossing where a task force of infantry and tanks was assembling preparatory to making a reconnaissance into Communist territory. Our front lines were then a couple of miles north of the river. The task force was to move toward the city of Chorwon, a big enemy supply-and-communications center ten miles beyond the front, with the object of seeing whether the Communists would offer any resistance to this probing advance, and, if so, where

15

and how. Should no resistance have been encountered by the time a certain point had been reached, the task force was to radio back asking for permission to continue on and reconnoitre Chorwon itself. If the task force were to enter the place, this might well be the big tactical news of the day, inasmuch as Chorwon represented one corner of a so-called "Iron Triangle" within which much of the enemy's materiel was thought to be located. The other corners were Hwachon and Kumhwa. By the time Hwachon fell to the Eighth Army, everybody in Korea had grown fond of the phrase, so a new Iron Triangle was proclaimed, with Pyonggang substituted for Hwachon.

Some two-thirds of the infantrymen selected for the expedition were replacements who had never previously seen combat. Lieutenant Colonel James H. Lee, of Dallas, Texas, was in charge of the outfit, which had, accordingly, been dubbed Task Force Lee. At the assembly point, the river, fifty yards wide, was spanned by a makeshift bridge some Army engineers had started putting across it the previous day. It was a single-track affair made of logs, planks, sandbags, stones, dirt, and American know-how. The engineers had worked on it until ten o'clock the night before, I learned when I arrived, and had returned at dawn to work on it some more. They were still working; a bulldozer was riding the middle, shoving dirt and stones around, in an effort to smooth the roadway. The bridge looked like a fragile support for the thirty-ton tanks that were set to lumber over it, but Army engineers have a knack of creating bridges of extraordinary staying power, and, indeed, the engineers themselves in Korea seemed to be considerably more durable than most mortals. A day earlier, for instance, I had visited a different spot along the same river and had admiringly watched six of them, chest-deep in water, struggling to put in place a crib that was to serve as part of the foundation for another bridge. I felt chilly, despite the full complement of clothing I was wearing, but the men in the stream, who were wearing only thin underwear and boots, kept at their damp and shivery toil for a solid hour without griping. If their mothers could have seen them, they'd probably have been appalled.

The bulldozer finally relinquished its perch on the bridge, and the elements of the task force began gingerly rolling across it. Colonel Lee and some other officers and men were standing at the north end of the bridge watching the procession go by. A captain told me that the infantrymen had risen at their bivouac area at four-thirty, had breakfast at five, boarded trucks at six-twenty, and reached the bridge

17

at seven-forty-five. They and their accompanying tanks, on which the foot soldiers were to ride as far as they could, had been split into three echelons and were to go forward in leapfrogging steps. Men from King Company, just then starting to move out, were to proceed to a predetermined spot and halt there to protect the rest of the force against ambush from the rear. Then Love Company and its tanks were to go on past King and assume defensive positions farther along toward Chorwon.

The last echelon, from Item Company, would wind up as the foremost one. "That is," the captain said, "if this damned bridge will hold out." He was not an engineer officer. He suggested that another corre- spondent, Sergeant Douglas DuBois, of *Stars & Stripes*, and I hang back and hitch a ride on one of the Item Company tanks, so that ultimately we could get a closeup view of the most forward action, if any.

It was nearly ten-thirty when DuBois and I hopped on the second in line of the last bunch of tanks to cross the bridge. Except for the crew inside, we were the only passengers aboard, but infantrymen were clustered on the tanks to our rear. We stood be- hind the turret, planting our feet amid a jumble of bedrolls, ration cases, shovels, and suitcases. Tank men are partial to suitcases, which, having handles,

18

can be more firmly moored to a bucking vehicle than some other kinds of luggage. Each of the tanks in Task Force Lee was manned by a crew of five—commander, loader, driver, assistant driver, and gunner —and armed with a 76-mm. cannon up front and a .50-calibre machine gun at the rear of the turret. It was a crisp, sunny morning, and the bare brown hills that flanked both edges of the valley up which we began traveling were faintly veiled with mist. The dirt road winding up through the valley was raised a bit above the level of the surrounding rice paddies, and its narrow shoulders sloped down into deep ditches. There hadn't been any rain for a few days, so the road was exceedingly dusty. The prevailing dryness, though, meant that the tanks could move over the paddies if they chose to, instead of having to stick to the road itself, as they are obliged to in Korea after even a brisk shower.

Our tank moved along in spurts, stopping whenever the tank ahead of us stopped. The column maintained an interval of some fifty yards between vehicles, just in case the Communists should pick that day to break out their still unrevealed air strength. Overhead, a couple of our light observation planes were flying as escorts; they would be handy for spotting anything we might be headed into. Pres-

19

ently, we came upon King Company and its tanks, deployed to our right and left. Soon after that, we rattled past a burned-out village where thirty or forty North Koreans were massed at the roadside. Their homes had been totally destroyed, but they were smiling, bowing, waving South Korean flags, and shouting, "*Mansai! Mansai!*"—the Korean equivalent of the Japanese *banzai*. I wondered aloud whether they viewed us as their liberators. Sergeant DuBois, a man more experienced in such matters, pointed out that Love Company must already have gone through there some time earlier.

Aside from our own strictly martial caravan, there were few sights or sounds to indicate that we were in a battle zone, but Sergeant DuBois said there undoubtedly were Chinese dug in on the hills at our flanks and our rear. There were the blackened ruins of the villages, to be sure, and some of the paddies were pitted with shell craters. In one ditch we saw a rusty Chinese rifle, and in another an abandoned Chinese truck. But that was about all. Before long, the tank commander got a radio message from the lead tank instructing us passengers to disembark and get on one of the infantry-laden tanks that were following us; it seemed that the two front tanks were supposed to draw whatever enemy fire there might be. So DuBois and I jumped off and squeezed in with a squad of soldiers clinging to the next tank in line.

At noon, we heard shots and saw some dust kick up about a quarter of a mile off to our right, and the column stopped. Practically nobody on a large battlefield ever knows precisely what's going on until after the fact; we would have had no idea what that flurry was if the sergeant commanding our tank hadn't relayed a radio message to us. "Some gooks bugged out across the field," he shouted. "They think we killed all of them." "That's what we're out here for— to kill the bastards," one of the infantrymen, a private first class carrying a walkie-talkie, remarked quietly. Not long after that, there were more shots. The column stopped again. Our tank's radio reported that the lead tank had been fired on. Over the walkie-talkie, almost simultaneously, came orders for the infantrymen to take to their feet. All of them scrambled down except one private, who had been assigned to man the tank's machine gun. One after another, the tanks in our echelon crawled off the road and spread out across the paddies on either side of it. Each infantry squad stuck close to the tank from which it had dismounted.

To our right, across the valley floor, was a village. Straight ahead was a series of ascending hills, with another village at the base of the foremost one. To the left was still another village, and a patrol of infantrymen started off warily to explore it. Not far from them, and only a bit ahead of the tanks, a burst of sparks and fleecy smoke rose from the ground. "White phosphorus," said the machine gunner, and, in the same breath, "Heard how yesterday's ball games came out?" I said I hadn't. "Probably our own artillery registering," he said, changing the subject back without changing the tone of his voice. Then there was silence, and since no orders were forthcoming over the radio, the crew climbed out of the tank and began opening ration cans for their lunch. DuBois and I joined them on the ground.

At twelve-thirty-five, word came to move on, and after we had hopped back on our tank, it progressed another two hundred yards. Then it stopped, and we heard planes. A flight of P-51s loomed up, dipped down as they approached the village directly ahead of us, and dropped bombs on it. They were napalm bombs. When they hit, fat cubes of blended flames and black smoke rose from the ground. After the air strike, we began to move forward again. There was rifle fire on our left flank. "Better open up on them guys on the hill," our tank commander said into his radio. "There's one laying right there in the brush." A

22

machine gun on one of the tanks on the left flank began a raking fire. There was intermittent return fire. The infantrymen with the tanks near ours took to a ditch between two paddies. For about five minutes, a good deal of firing went on, and during the densest of it an old Korean man strolled serenely up the road, heading toward the bombed village, from which clouds of black smoke were still billowing. When the hubbub died down, the machine gunner on our tank said, "You know, I'd rather be down there in the ditch with the other boys than up here. Once you get with a crowd of good boys, you like to stay with them." There were some more sporadic rifle shots. Then our tank commander, who had been surveying the countryside through binoculars, said he had spotted a bunker on one of the hills ahead of us, twenty-three hundred yards away, and a couple of people moving around its entrance. Over his radio, the sergeant asked for permission to put a few rounds into it. "Fire at will," came the reply. He fired three rounds, each time courteously notifying his passengers topside when he was about to let fly, so we wouldn't be surprised by the noise, which we assuredly would have been if we hadn't been alerted for it. The third round landed square on the bunker, and the sergeant, with reasonable pride in this dis-

23

play of marksmanship, let DuBois and me borrow his glasses, so we could examine the smoke pouring out of it.

There was another explosion over to our left, a little ahead of our tanks. "Sounds like our own artillery landing short," the machine-gunner told me. "Our people must be calling for fire on the gooks in the village ahead." I was still reflecting on how much better a grasp he seemed to have of the situation than I had when there were two more blasts as shells landed a few hundred yards off, close to the tanks on the left. "Incoming," said the tank commander laconically. I glanced around and noticed that all the infantrymen were in ditches. DuBois and I headed for a ditch ourselves, with the machine-gunner from our tank at our heels. "That fifty's gonna have to fire itself for a while," he said.

Shells were bursting in fairly rapid succession now. Somebody must have transmitted an order to the tanks, for all at once they turned around and began withdrawing through the paddies. It felt lonely, sitting in the ditch, separated from their bulky protectiveness. A moment later, the foot soldiers received word to pull back, and they took off across the paddies after the tanks, alternately running and walking fast, and crouching or flopping down when-

24

ever they heard the swoosh or the burst of a shell. DuBois and I tagged along after them. Making our way across one paddy, we saw some safe-conduct passes lying on the ground—the kind the United Nations forces had been bombarding the enemy with, in the hope of influencing them to surrender. "I wish I had a safe-conduct pass myself right now," gasped DuBois, without breaking his stride, a long one. The tanks had stopped after pulling back some four hundred yards, and I sat down, panting, next to the reassuring solidity of what I had come to think of as my tank. DuBois and the infantrymen kept on going across the paddies until they were practically out of sight.

Six of our jet planes whined through the sky, wheeled, dived, and dropped some more napalm on an area where the annoying guns were evidently thought to be emplaced. The tank commander called to me that one of our observation planes had detected two self-propelled guns in there. The enemy firing ceased while the jets were working the place over, but as soon as they had left, it started up again. "By God, they haven't got him yet," the tank commander said. Three more rounds fell in over at the left. "Those sound like mortars," he added.

The firing stopped. I looked at my watch; it was

25

two-thirty. The air cleared of smoke, and our tanks, strung across the fields, looked as undisturbed as if they were on a maneuver. Over the tank radio came the order, "Move out." "Well," said the commander when he had passed this word along, "maybe we'll get back in time for early chow." I climbed aboard the tank, and we headed back to the road and floundered up onto it. When we reached a command post Colonel Lee had set up, I got off. A full colonel was standing there. "It was good for those replacements to come under fire," he told me gravely, "but it was the worst thing possible for them to have to withdraw under artillery fire. I wish we'd been allowed to keep pushing forward, as we could have if we hadn't had a limited objective. These troops have got to learn that when artillery falls, the best thing is to advance under it." I asked him what he thought the enemy had been throwing at us. "Two self-propelleds and a battery of artillery," he said. I asked about the mortars. "No mortars," he said flatly.

Then I chatted for a minute with Colonel Lee. He said that the day had been a success to the extent that the task force had ascertained the point beyond which the Communists were determined not to let us advance without a fight and to the extent that four enemy soldiers had been killed—the ones who had been fired on earlier in the day as they lit out across the field. He said our side had suffered no casualties except some broken glass in the periscope of one tank, which had come close to being hit by a mortar shell. "Were they using mortars, then?" I asked. He nodded emphatically.

I hitched a jeep ride back to the divisional command post, arriving there at about five. The bridge over the river was in better shape than it had been in the morning; the engineers were still working on it. I imagine the infantrymen got back to their camp site a little later than I got back to mine, though probably not too late for evening chow. That night, at division headquarters, an intelligence officer, summarizing the day's activities in general, disposed of the task force in relatively short order by saying merely that it had gone out, reconnoitred, and run into fifty rounds of self-propelled artillery and mortar fire. The next day I saw the Eighth Army communiqué covering the appropriate period. "A task force probing the area south of Chorwon received some artillery fire," it read. As far as the official record is concerned, that is probably all that will ever be remembered about Task Force Lee.

3

OF ALL the capital cities of the world, Seoul, once a bustling metropolis with a population of a million and a half, has had the most turbulent recent history. In the nine months following June, 1950, when it was the governmental seat of the Republic of Korea, it changed hands four times, falling to the North Koreans three days after the fighting began, being reoccupied in late September by the United Nations forces, falling to the Communists again on January 4th, and in mid-March being taken from them once more. When I paid my first visit to Seoul, a few weeks after that, it was still a comfortable distance

28

behind the front lines, and things were still fairly quiet, but even then it was apparent that its status could shift another time or two, and, perhaps to remind the residents of this possibility, a sentry I saw stationed at the entrance to one South Korean military installation had a machine gun mounted on a table in front of him, its muzzle pointing north.

It is always hard to estimate with any accuracy the extent of a city's ruin, but people who had made a thorough check-up of Seoul after its reoccupation by the United Nations in the spring told me they considered it fifty per cent destroyed. It was just about as inert as a city could become, short of altogether ceasing to exist. Its streets were bare of traffic, except for the military vehicles rattling along them; its buildings were burned and shattered; and the forsythia and azaleas then bursting into bloom seemed awfully inappropriate to their dismal setting. Damaged or not, Seoul has long been the mecca of Korea, and it was important to Koreans, or at any rate South Koreans, not only that the city should continue to exist but that the Republic's flag should fly above the National Assembly Building. (The same colors were on display at numerous flag stalls that had sprung up amid the rubble. A cynical Korean I talked to told me, however, that some of these stalls

29

were stocking the Communist colors, too, for surreptitious sale to those citizens who might want to be prepared for any eventuality.)

President Rhee's government had remained down south at Pusan, where it had been holding forth since its second hasty departure from Seoul, and it was to stay there for a while longer, as the former capital, in addition to having become extremely uncomfortable, was regarded as part of a tactical area. Early in April, it was being run by a couple of hundred municipal officials, who had just returned to it, and by an American team of seven Army officers, eleven enlisted men, and four civilians, all belonging to an outfit called the United Nations Civil Assistance Command in Korea, or, to use the inevitable abbreviation, UNCACK. (They had to abandon the city again, for a while, late in April, when the enemy advanced to within a few miles of its perimeter in a not far from successful attempt to retake it once more.) They had quite a job on their hands. Seoul had no electric power, except that furnished by portable generators; no water, except what could be drawn from twenty-five hundred wells providentially located within the city limits; no communications, except Signal Corps telephones; and no public transportation whatever. Each time an occupying power had

decamped, it had taken with it all operating transport, either to prevent it from serving the opposition
or to carry evacuees. There were still usable trolley
tracks on the main thoroughfares, but Seoul's streetcars had been so burned and bombed and battered
that only ninety-six of them were sturdy enough to
warrant reconditioning. Even if these had been re-
conditioned, they couldn't have been used, for want
of trolley wires. And even if there had been trolley
wires, the lack of electricity would have kept the cars
immobile.

When the North Koreans first invaded Seoul, less
than a hundred thousand of the city's peacetime residents left it. When the Chinese came in in January,
all but a couple of hundred thousand demonstrated
their distaste for them by pulling out. Something like
half a million of these migrated to islands off the
southern tip of the peninsula. According to the South
Korean municipal administration, which had taken
some censuses that, in view of the city's paralyzed
state, would seem to have been miraculously precise,
there were 134,045 people living in Seoul on March
14th, when the first Republic of Korea patrols re-
entered the city. By April 16th, an up-to-the-minute
tabulation that was brought to my attention showed
that the number had risen to 442,953. Considering

that these folk had had to come back by foot, it was an astounding influx.

Below the Han River, the three-hundred-yard-wide, fifteen-foot-deep stream that flows along the southern edge of the city and over which, while it was frozen during the winter, thousands of refugees trudged toward the south, I saw lines of homeward-bound Koreans, bent under bundles that contained everything they owned, stretching back for miles. Every night, from five to ten thousand of them were straggling back across the Han, despite the fact that the authorities were trying to deter them by means of barbed wire strung along the river banks and armed guards posted on the pontoon bridges our engineers had thrown across the river. It was explained to me that there were two primary reasons for this inhospitable attitude. In the first place, if the Communists were to take Seoul again, all the people who were trying to get back in might have to be re-evacuated, which, even if they were to proceed under their own power, would create bad traffic and feeding problems. In the second, because of the sorry condition Seoul was in, any increase in population constituted increased health and fire hazards. The waterworks were not functioning, and the municipal fire-fighting equipment was in deplorable shape. A month before, there hadn't been a single fire engine in the city, and the first fire that broke out after the South Koreans moved back in, a small one that under normal circumstances could have been doused in short order, leveled fifty houses. By the time the population rose again to nearly half a million, the city had five pieces of equipment, which was better than nothing but, even so, less than what often turns out to battle a brush fire at, say, Scarborough-on-the-Hudson.

Koreans are thought by some Americans to be exceptionally stolid and unemotional, but sentiment appeared to be an important factor in the determination of the citizens of Seoul to return to their city, for on the surface there was little to go back to. Few homes were entirely undamaged, and many had been razed. Even with less than a third of the city's customary population on the scene, there was a good deal of overcrowding in those houses that were habitable. Fortunately, Koreans never have gone in much for furniture—they habitually sleep on the floor—or for sanitation, so it proved easier to double up there than it might be in fussier parts of the world. No business was being conducted in the city, and there was no work for anyone other than those citizens employed by the United Nations forces or

33

the local government. The only public eating place open in the entire city was a tea-shop. A dance-hall proprietor, apparently unaware that Seoul had been declared off limits to all military personnel except those having official business in it, had bravely re-opened his establishment, but the occasion was a flop, since there were practically no soldiers on hand, and no music or girls, either.

Those South Koreans who returned to Seoul were relieved to find intact the city's celebrated bell, a huge bronze affair that is around five hundred years old. It weighs about sixty tons, which seemed to be the principal reason neither side had carted it off. The bell was resting on the ground in approximately the center of the old walled city of Seoul. Before the war, when it hung in a pagoda, it used to be rung every evening at sundown, when the gates were closed for the night. Legend has it that two or three earlier bells were cast, all paid for by public subscription. Each of the earlier ones cracked before it could be put into service. Finally, the only citizen of Seoul who hadn't contributed to the enterprise, a penniless widow with an infant child, decided that her remiss-ness was the jinx, and she did her bit by dropping her baby into the molten metal out of which the newest bell was to be fashioned. The result was a fine, un-

34

cracked bell, which is said to have a tone resembling the cry of a child calling for its mother. The bell hasn't been heard much lately. Its pagoda burned down during the summer of 1950, and the bell dropped to the ground. It had been hoisted up on a temporary scaffold that October, when it was rung in celebration of United Nations Day, but it had been lowered to the ground again afterward and hadn't pealed since.

The Chinese have been less harsh in their treatment of prisoners of war, by and large, than the North Koreans, and the second, Chinese, occupation of Seoul, similarly, was less severe than the first Communist rule of the city. It was hardly gentle, however. Shortly before being driven out, the Communists issued an order requiring all males between fifteen and thirty and all females between sixteen and twenty-five to accompany their retreating troops to the north. According to a police report, forty-one thousand South Koreans were whisked off as a consequence of this stern directive—the men, it was commonly thought, to be used in combat against their own people, and the women to serve in labor battalions and as human mine detectors. A lot of the citizens of Seoul who weren't in these age groups failed to survive the occupation anyway, dying as a result of cold, starvation,

35

or United Nations air raids. No one I talked to could say with any degree of certainty how many such casualties there were, since many of the victims were presumably buried. The South Korean police had been making a house-to-house check of the city, though, and in five weeks had counted nearly fifteen hundred unburied bodies, including, surprisingly, corpses of both Chinese and North Korean soldiers who had starved to death themselves. Relatively few people, I was told, had been executed, or even arrested, for their political leanings, and just as the second occupation by the North had been the more clement in this respect, so had been the second occupation by the South. I was also told that some of the Republic of Korea police who had energetically seized and disposed of alleged pro-Communists between September and January, with little regard for any recognized principles of justice, were back at their posts, but that this time they, too, were acting much more restrained.

While the United Nations troops were south of the Han in March, preparing to re-enter Seoul, rumors reached them of terrible epidemics within the city. The first civil-assistance officers to cross the river were amazed to find not only that there were no epidemics raging but that the health situation was, all things considered, much better than it had any right to be. They discovered a few cases of smallpox and typhoid, and, since the place was swarming with children, some chicken pox and measles, but nothing resembling an epidemic. Still, as a precaution, every Korean who could be rounded up was vaccinated, inoculated, and liberally sprinkled with DDT. For the first few days, children were practically the only residents of Seoul to show their faces. Then, gradually, the very old, the only other group around in substantial numbers, emerged from the hiding places they had burrowed into while waiting to see who would win what they hoped would be the last struggle for their much-fought-over community. Seoul also proved to be harboring a number of five-man guerrilla teams left behind by the Communists to harass their successors, but after these had killed a couple of policemen all were apprehended, or at least it was thought that all were. Of the children, it was estimated that at least four thousand of them were homeless and penniless orphans, many of whom roamed the streets and alleys in skulking and scavenging packs. There was no one to look after the majority of them; perhaps one-tenth of them had been rounded up and installed in makeshift orphanages. Ultimately, quite a few were shipped out of

37

Seoul and to other orphanages scattered around the country. (One such establishment that I subsequently visited in Taegu was set up in a botanical garden, with greenhouses converted into classrooms and dormitories.) Korean children, if they hoped to survive the war, had to become exceedingly self-reliant and resourceful; even the orphanages could often provide them barely with enough to subsist on. The United Nations forces did a lot to help the orphanages keep going, but nonetheless there were needs that went unfilled—such as the need of one institution for, as expressed in a hopeful announcement, "small and medium crutches."

Rice is, of course, the staple of the Korean diet, usually supplemented by "side foods"—mostly fish, garlic and red peppers, and seaweed. To sustain the inhabitants it found in Seoul, UNCACK set up a station to distribute rice in each of the city's two hundred and ninety-two *dongs,* a *dong* being a sector of two or three square blocks. The rice, much of it donated by Thailand and the Philippines, was shipped to the seaport of Inchon, seventeen miles from Seoul, and taken in by trucks. Adults were receiving slightly more than a pound of rice apiece daily, and children, invalids, nursing mothers, and pregnant women got a little more, and a milk ration as well. Moreover, to make possible the purchasing of side foods, each citizen was getting fifty *won* a day, which is the equivalent of a fraction less than one cent. Considering the shortage of produce, food prices were astonishingly low at the half-dozen markets that were open. The scarcity of money was the reason. The venders who presided over the makeshift stalls were supposed to provide their customers with receipts attesting to their rightful ownership of the goods they were offering, but to judge by some of the wares on display—American Army rations, cigarettes, and toilet articles, for instance—it seemed not wholly unlikely that the matter of a formal receipt was sometimes being overlooked.

Only at the markets were any appreciable number of Koreans visible; in the absence of any other kind of community life in Seoul, the market place had become more than ever the center of group activity. Men, women, and children would hang around the stalls for hours on end, examining, though not often buying, such assorted merchandise as shoes, mirrors, firewood, kimonos, straw baskets, chinaware, teakwood boxes, sterling-silver tea sets, neckties, abacuses, clay urns, parasols, postcards, and hot and cold seaweed. Hardly anywhere else in Seoul did I get the impression that the city was much more than

39

a ghost town, but here and there I came upon a sign
of the affection that its citizens still felt for it, no
matter at how low an ebb its fortunes might be. It
was perhaps typical of what Seoul means to most
Koreans that one day there I saw two old women who
were industriously scrubbing dirt off the brick façade
of a building, notwithstanding the fact that all the
rest of the building lay in a crumpled heap on the
other side of the façade.

4

SOLDIER humor is often wry and often topical, and it was therefore not surprising, as the Korean battle lines shifted back and forth across the Thirty-eighth Parallel, that a popular jest among the G.I.s had it that eligibility for rotation was to be determined by the number of times a man had crossed the Parallel— three points per crossing being the usual sardonic recommendation. If such a system existed, a lot of Americans would have earned credits during the spring of 1951, when just before the big Communist offensive began practically all our combat forces were deployed north of the Parallel and after it ended

41

practically all of them were well south of it. In discussions about rotation it was also noted, not altogether laughingly, that inasmuch as no Chinese were known to have traversed the Parallel when the North Koreans started the whole seesaw business, and inasmuch as the North Koreans themselves were not too seriously involved in the spring push, the doubtful distinction of having accumulated the maximum number of points—fifteen was the figure generally agreed upon at the time—might belong exclusively, in a sense, to Joseph Stalin, who probably had no desire to be shifted from his assignment.

The United Nations military authorities, regardless of how much back-pedaling the troops under them had to do, frowned upon the use of the word "retreat," and preferred such less upsetting words as "displacement." So persistently was this equivocation espoused that it came to be used perhaps even more universally than the authorities intended: one night, in the middle of a brisk skirmish, I heard a junior officer report to a senior that the enemy in front of their position had displaced. (The frequent displacement of one side or the other from a spot it had occupied gave rise to certain humorous observations, too. One naval officer at Inchon, where both sides had made use of the same barracks during their alternating tenancies of the port, remarked that the next time he had to evacuate the city, he planned to tack to a barracks wall a sign saying, "Please leave these premises, as a courtesy to later occupants, in the same condition in which you find them.") Official feelings about terminology notwithstanding, it would have been improper to characterize the United Nations withdrawal that followed the Communist assault as a retreat. Except in the case of several units that were encircled by masses of Chinese and had to try to get out as best they could, the move to the rear was exceptionally orderly, and in sharp contrast to the southward trek of the previous winter. Then, the U.N. forces had been obliged to abandon or destroy a good deal of equipment; our Air Force, for instance, had to set fire to thousands of gallons of precious gasoline that, only a week or so before, it had gone to considerable pains to fly to advance landing strips from bases in Japan. In the spring the situation was, in general, quite different. When a single and relatively expendable two-and-a-half-ton truck belonging to the Turkish Brigade broke down and couldn't be repaired with any parts that were on hand, the Turks, instead of leaving it by the roadside, brought up a tank and conscientiously towed it south with them. Around the clock, for days and nights on end, there was a nearly bumper-to-bumper procession of United Nations vehicles traveling down the north-south roads of the peninsula. The sight, under pleasanter circumstances, could have made a homesick New Yorker think of the West Side Highway on a Sunday evening in spring.

As our troops pulled back to a defense line that, on the west, was only a few miles north of Seoul, they were once again given impressive evidence of the way a free election would undoubtedly have gone if one could have been held among the permanent residents of the country. Both above and below the Parallel, out of the hills and valleys that to American patrols had appeared to be no longer populated, Korean families emerged, joined with others at the crossroads of the well-packed dirt paths that run atop the dikes separating the paddies, and began plodding south in further round-the-clock columns. They didn't seem to know exactly where they were going, but they obviously didn't want to end up any place where the Communists might be going. One morning not long after this new mobile phase of the war started, I happened to be poking around a village through which one of these columns was passing. A middle-aged woman, with a nursing child at her breast, a slightly older one on her back, and a big

44

bundle on her head, trudged by, and as she did she glanced over at a convoy of trucks rolling along a nearby road. "Pusan," she said matter-of-factly, referring to a point more than two hundred miles distant.

Whether this woman had in mind a potential destination for the Eighth Army or for herself, I had no idea, but if she was reflecting on the military picture, she was more pessimistic by a long sight than the proprietors of that fleet of trucks. In less than a week, to be sure, the Chinese, who traveled on foot themselves, had gained almost fifty miles, but as an intelligence officer on the western front put it at about the forty-five-mile stage, "There's no sweat. We've got plenty of time and plenty of territory." General Van Fleet, the chief proprietor, was the least pessimistic of anybody. Running into him in Seoul one day while the Communists were within artillery range of the place, and while our own artillery was firing from inside the city in an attempt to keep them from getting within, say, mortar range, I asked Van Fleet if he thought he would have to evacuate Seoul. "No," he replied, emphatically. And he proved, of course, to be right. It was hard to guess just what the Communists hoped to gain by their big push. Undoubtedly they aspired to re-enter the capital triumphantly

45

on or about the first of May. To judge from the battle cry one Chinese outfit was shrilly uttering as it rushed upon an American infantry company one night— "Kill G.I.s!"—a primary objective would seem to have been not unlike one General Ridgway had from time to time stressed to his troops: to kill as many of the enemy as possible. The trouble was that there were so many of the enemy. The Chinese didn't always attack in formations massive enough to warrant the designation of "human sea," a phrase that was much used, and perhaps sometimes overused, during the spring months (the enemy once astonished the United Nations press corps, which felt that it had kind of a monopoly on "human sea," by employing the term self-descriptively themselves), but it was far from uncommon for two enemy divisions to attack one of our battalions, and two Chinese battalions one of our platoons. "They breed them faster than we can kill them," one G.I. said. Similarly, a medical officer who in civilian life specialized in obstetrics remarked, in a filial letter to his mother, that he could not help noting with professional interest that, notwithstanding the awesome mechanization of his own side, the female pelvis was proving to be a dismayingly effective weapon.

Some of the Chinese in action, while quite some

46

time removed from the womb, were certainly in their military infancy. Prisoners were taken who had been in the army only a month and had had only four days' training before being put in the lines—in several instances, armed with no more than a bayonet and a few hand grenades. Those thus scantily equipped would generally be in the second or third echelon of an assault force. It was their superiors' notion that by the time they reached the line of battle they'd be able to scrounge additional weapons from the dead or wounded lying around there, who had, initially, been much better schooled and outfitted. It was the firm conviction of many of our own infantrymen that many of the enemy, regardless of echelon, were doped up. Some G.I. or another was always telling of finding on Chinese bodies hypodermic syringes and packets of a soluble white powder. Certainly a considerable number of the live Chinese, and especially the neophytes among them, seemed far from clear as to what they were supposed to be doing, and this was not out of plain backwardness, for according to our interrogators of prisoners only about one-tenth of them were illiterate. Several prisoners claimed that they didn't know what company they belonged to, and some said that they didn't even know that they were in Korea and thought they were fighting the

Chinese Nationalists somewhere or other. Other prisoners, however, asserted that they received thorough political indoctrination—two hours of it daily, one man declared. In some enemy units, there was a political instructor for every platoon. A group of our infantrymen were flabbergasted, in the course of nabbing one Communist who was crouched in a foxhole absorbed in a newspaper, to discover that the paper was the *Daily Worker*. They asked him if he could read English. "No, you sons of bitches," he replied, employing what in an abnormally masculine part of the world was, of course, excellent English.

There were recurrent rumors in Korea about extremely young soldiers fighting among the Chinese, but one team of interrogators who had talked with several thousand prisoners told me that the youngest they'd run into—and he was a notable exception—had been sixteen, by Chinese reckoning, or fourteen, by ours. Most of the Chinese were between eighteen and twenty-four, American-style age. Around ninety per cent of them had come from farms; since only about eighty per cent of the Chinese people are farmers, this might indicate that the Communists had done their most energetic recruiting in rural areas. Among one group of prisoners I checked on, quite a few hadn't been home since 1945, and some had had no word from home, not even a postcard, in five years.

48

While in Korea, moreover, they received no news whatever from China. They had no access to newspapers nor to radios. I asked if they ever protested about this, and part of the answer, a negative one, furnished a good example of the importance of maintaining face in the Orient. "If our officers knew we had any complaints," was the reply, "we might be criticized in front of other soldiers." These men all readily asserted that their leaders were active Communists; they denied with equal readiness that they themselves were. Many of them sought earnestly to identify themselves as former members of the Chinese Nationalist Army who had been conscripted, involuntarily, into the theoretically volunteer ranks of the Chinese Communist Forces—or, as American soldiers often referred to them, translating "C.C.F." into the Army alphabet, the "Charlie Charlie Foxes." The Chinese seemed as anxious to dissociate themselves from the Communist Party, after being captured, as many Germans seemed, after the Second World War, to dissociate themselves from the Nazi Party. Some of the Chinese in our prisoner-of-war camps appeared not especially eager to go back to their homes at the conclusion of hostilities. This reluctance was particularly evident in the case of amputees and others who had been permanently maimed. Apparently they felt that life in China, in the post-Korean War years, would be a

49

question of the survival of the fittest, and that men who couldn't help themselves stood little chance of getting any help from anyone else.

During their spring offensives, the Communists used comparatively little artillery and almost no aircraft, and since the United Nations were efficiently equipped with both in large measure, the enemy elected to do most of their fighting at night, when their movements could not be observed too well until they were nearly on top of our troops. During the daytime, our lines would be carefully pulled back, wherever possible by vehicle. While we were withdrawing during the day, the enemy would follow right along, not even stopping under murderous air and artillery assaults but moving unfalteringly past mounting heaps of their own casualties. As each night approached, we would establish defensive positions. Presently, after dark, would come the bugle calls and colored lights that signified the imminence of a Chinese attack, and a little while after that, regardless of how much artillery or mortar or machine-gun fire might be in the way, the charge. Because of the numerical mismatching that prevailed, not even the most resolute group of United Nations soldiers could be certain of holding its positions, and our lines would crack, to the dismay of the people behind them. Battalion and regimental command posts, ordinarily spots incomparably safer than a company or platoon headquarters, were on several occasions subjected to small-arms fire, and even divisional command posts were bothered by infiltrating Chinese. And the fighting didn't invariably cease at sunrise. At daybreak one morning, I was chatting with a captain at a battalion command post, where we had spent an uneasy night, owing to the presence somewhere near it of around five hundred Chinese, who, eight hours earlier, had overrun one of the battalion's companies a mile and a half from our position. The captain, gratefully watching the hills in front of us become increasingly visible—now and then a few enemy soldiers could actually be seen with the naked eye, silhouetted against the lightening sky as they darted along the crest of a ridge—remarked that he surely was getting fed up with the routine the Chinese had imposed on him. "I used to say 'Another day, another dollar' at night," he told me jocularly, "but now I say it in the morning." A couple of minutes later, almost as if to point up the danger of making any kind of flat statement about a war, a Chinese machine gun opened up on the command post and the captain was instantly killed by a shot through the neck.

51

5

IT IS hard to tell which battles of the Korean War military historians will ultimately single out for special mention, but it is doubtful whether they can overlook one two-and-a-half-day engagement that, whatever name the historians may settle on for it, is known to those who went through it as the Battle of the Imjin, and that has already been officially characterized as "epic" by the Eighth Army. The battle began, just south of the Imjin River and some twenty-five miles northwest of Seoul, on the night of April 22nd, as the Chinese were launching their spring offensive all across the front, and it continued, without letup, until midafternoon of April 25th. The great majority of the United Nations troops who participated in it were British, of the 29th Brigade, but it was nonetheless a fittingly multinational affair, involving Belgians, South Koreans, and Filipinos, as well as Americans from both the continental United States and Puerto Rico. The 29th Brigade, with a total strength of sixty-six hundred and a front-line fighting strength of four thousand, suffered more than a thousand casualties during that bloody span of time. In return, it inflicted a vastly larger number of casualties on the enemy; the exact count is indefinite, inasmuch as the British decline to assume credit for killing anybody unless they have actually seen him dead. They saw a great many dead Chinese those two and a half days, being frequently in hand-to-hand contention with the enemy, and on occasion, to conserve ammunition, being under orders to hold their fire until their attackers were only fifteen yards away. Out of something like sixty thousand Chinese who assaulted the seventeen-thousand-yard sector the brigade was holding when the battle started, it is widely, if unofficially, believed that between ten and fifteen thousand were dispatched. And what is perhaps more important—since hordes of dead Chinese were almost as commonplace as hordes of live ones

53

in Korea that particular week—is that the steadfast resistance of the British to this massive assault was very likely the most influential single factor in the dashing of the Communists' probable hope of celebrating May Day in the capital city of the Republic of Korea.

The entire 29th Brigade saw action in the Battle of the Imjin, but the worst assault fell upon one unit, the 1st Battalion of the Gloucestershire Regiment, informally called the Glosters. Of the six hundred and twenty-two Glosters who were in the most advanced of the brigade's three echelons when the fight got under way, just five officers and thirty-four other ranks were available for duty three days afterward, and they only because they had made a near-miraculous withdrawal through enemy fire so intense and enveloping that they subsequently said they felt like human targets in a shooting gallery. Their commanding officer, a tall, taciturn, pipe-smoking lieutenant colonel named J. P. Carne, who has served with the Glosters since 1925, is missing in action, as is his regimental sergeant major, E. J. Hobbs, whose association with the outfit goes back equally far. When, on the morning of the twenty-fifth, the Glosters were so hard pressed and so inextricably cut off from all other friendly troops that they could no longer function as an effective fighting force, every man was authorized to break through the encircling Chinese as best he could. The Colonel and the Sergeant Major elected to stay with the wounded, along with the Glosters' medical officer and chaplain. The handful of Glosters who did get out brought back several versions of Colonel Carne's last words to them. The one most generally accepted is that as they took leave of him, and as he stood there among the sad and suffering remnants of the organization to which practically his entire adult life had been devoted, he said, with the perfect discipline for which his soldiering country-men have long been noted, "Any of you chaps happen to have a spare twist of tobacco?"

The 29th Brigade, which arrived in Korea early in November, is composed of a number of units with ancient traditions, among them the 1st Battalion, Royal Ulster Rifles; the 1st Battalion, Royal North-umberland Fusiliers; the 45th Field Regiment, Royal Artillery; and the 8th King's Royal Irish Hussars, this last a cavalry outfit that was formed in 1693 and took part in the Charge of the Light Brigade at Balaklava, but is now mechanized and equipped with fifty-two-ton tanks called Centurions. The Ulster Rifles, who wear as a device the harp of Ireland and the crown of Britain, had a rough time early in January in the brigade's one other costly action in Korea; two hundred and thirty of them were killed. This loss happened to occur in the very area assigned to the 29th Brigade in mid-April, and on their return to the unhappily familiar scene, the Rifles reburied some of their dead who had fallen there, and commissioned a stonemason in Seoul to cut an obelisk to mark the spot. Dedication of the monument was scheduled for April 23rd, but the ceremonies were, perforce, postponed. April 23rd is a big day for the British. Not only is it Shakespeare's birthday but it is also the day consecrated to their patron saint, Saint George. To the Northumberland Fusiliers, who trace their martial lineage back to 1674, the holiday is especially precious, for Saint George and his dragon are represented on the badge they wear on their berets. They had planned a turkey dinner for the twenty-third, and had fitted themselves out with the red and white roses (made of cloth, on this occasion) that are the traditional cap ornaments for the day. The banquet had to be canceled, but the Fusiliers wore their roses anyway. Some of the gunners of the Royal Artillery joined the battle sporting real roses, which they had had flown in from Japan for the holiday. But they, too, were unable to pay any further tribute to Saint George. While the battle was on, they were busy

56

firing more rounds per weapon—the average was a thousand—than had been hurled even at El Alamein, theretofore considered the biggest show ever put on by British artillerymen. The Royal Artillery motto is *"Ubique,"* and its guns in this case were twenty-five pounders, mounted to permit a traverse of three hundred and sixty degrees, and during the Battle of the Imjin, with Chinese assaulting some of the gun emplacements from the rear, they had to be traversed full circle. The guns have a range of thirteen miles; they were fired point-blank, over open sights, at enemy riflemen fifty yards off. Toward the end of the battle, every round of twenty-five-pound ammunition in Korea had been delivered to the British gun positions, and lorries were waiting at two airstrips for a fresh supply that had been urgently ordered from Japan. But the battle was over before the ammunition ran out.

As for the Glosters, they date back to 1694 and have acquired forty-four battle honors—more than any other British regiment. The men of the 1st Battalion—the only element of the regiment in Korea— probably earned a forty-fifth at the Imjin, and they have already been awarded an American citation for their stand there. The Glosters have streamers on their regimental colors for Waterloo, Sevastopol, and

Gallipoli, among other legendary arenas, and General Wolfe is said to have died in the arms of a Gloster during the Battle of Quebec. On March 21, 1801, while arrayed against the French at Alexandria, the Glosters, who then fought in geometric rows, were surrounded, and received the order "Rear rank, right-about face and fire!" They battled back-to-back until the French were driven off, and ever since then the members of the regiment have been entitled to wear two cap badges, one in front and one in back. They are the only British troops who enjoy this privilege. The men who were to fight virtually back-to-back again, just a month after the hundred-and-fiftieth anniversary of their most cherished day, were for the most part experienced soldiers, many of them reservists with wives and children, who were recalled to service a year ago. Their average age was over thirty. At five minutes to eight on the morning of April 25th, when, after fighting almost without food or water or sleep for nearly sixty hours, these Glosters reported to brigade headquarters that their radio was about to run out of power and that they would appreciate having some air and artillery missiles dropped thirty yards from their own position, the brigade commander, a normally unbending brigadier, had a special message relayed to them. "No one but the Glosters could have done it," it said.

During the daytime of April 22nd, there were no particular signs of trouble to come. All along the front, to be sure, the United Nations had for several days been awaiting the Chinese offensive, but no one could anticipate precisely when it would be launched, nor did the British seem more or less likely than any other troops in the line to bear the brunt of the attack. On the twenty-first, the British, who had the 1st Republic of Korea Division on their left and the American 3rd Infantry Division on their right, had sent an exploratory patrol across the Imjin. It had traveled ten thousand yards beyond the river and had encountered only a scattering of enemy troops. A British intelligence report took note of a "large undetermined number of enemy north of the river," but concluded that nothing more worrisome than strong enemy probing patrols could be expected on the twenty-third and twenty-fourth. The brigade troops in the line were getting hot meals and, assuming that they would continue to get them, had no combat rations along. That turned out to be unfortunate, for the most any one of them had to eat during the battle was one hard-boiled egg and a slice of bread. As it soon developed, not only were the Chinese ready to undertake far more than probing patrols, but the ones on the Glosters' front were an exceptionally well-outfitted bunch of Chinese. They had new uniforms, ample rations, new Russian weapons in prime condition, and new shoes. One enemy soldier who was taken prisoner even had a spare pair of new shoes, made in Shanghai, a most unusual luxury for a Chinese infantryman—or, for that matter, a British or American infantryman—in combat. But it is to be doubted whether all the soldiers facing the brigade were as sharp as their equipment. During the battle, for instance, one Gloster rifleman saw two Chinese sitting in plain view on a ridge six hundred yards distant, eating lunch. He shot one of them, and the man toppled over. The other, scarcely a foot away, didn't even glance at the victim, but placidly went on eating.

In any event, the brigade's orders from above committed it to holding its positions, no matter what opposition might be forthcoming. On the eve of the battle, a battalion of Belgians attached to the British was deployed just north of the Imjin, on the brigade's right. Behind the river were the Fusiliers. On the left were the Glosters, in an especially rugged area, four miles broad, dotted with sheer rock cliffs rising to a height of two hundred and fifty feet. The Ulster Rifles were in reserve. The weather was clear on the twenty-second, as it was to be throughout the battle, but things were so quiet during the day that only one supporting air strike was asked of the United States Air Force and Navy fliers backing up the brigade. At six o'clock in the evening, the Belgians were attacked and almost immediately cut off; four hours later, the Fusiliers were hit. A patrol from the Rifles set off to aid the Belgians but couldn't reach them, and for most of that first night the Belgians were the main objects of concern. They stayed in their ticklish situation for another twenty-four hours, in the course of which a tank column tried, and failed, to get to them; on the night of the twenty-third, they managed to slide over to the right flank and sneak out, with relatively few casualties.

Shortly after midnight of the twenty-second, when Saint George's Day was only half an hour old, Able Company of the Glosters was attacked. By four o'clock, the whole battalion was engaged, and by six the whole brigade. The enemy came in three waves. In the first rush, Able Company lost its commander and two other officers. One walkie-talkie operator, running out of ammunition, used his rifle as a club, swinging it at the Chinese as they came into his foxhole and shouting, "*Banzai*, you bastards! *Banzai!*" A

61

few minutes later, the radioman regained his hereditary reserve and called into his transmitter, with finality, "We're overrun. We've had it. Cheerio." By midmorning, the Glosters had at least a regiment in front of them and, because the South Koreans on their left had been driven back several thousand yards, an indefinite number on the hills behind them. By midday, the Glosters hadn't been budged from the high points they had instructions to hold, but they were completely separated from the rest of the brigade, and the Chinese had penetrated so far back that the battalion's supply echelon was overrun, too, and nine of its men were taken prisoner. Quantities of the things the Glosters needed most desperately—machine guns, ammunition, and medical supplies—were packed into straw-lined bags and dropped to them by six light observation planes. A larger-scale airdrop was set up for the following morning. At dawn on the twenty-fourth, three Flying Boxcars were poised high over the Glosters' positions, waiting for the morning mist to lift so they could descend close enough to drop their cargo accurately. But when the mist rose, the pilots found the Glosters, and not a few Chinese, fighting literally inside a curtain of falling shells that the brigade's gunners and mortarmen were throwing around them. The planes couldn't dip down unless the shelling was halted, and the decision was up to the Glosters. The Glosters waved the hovering Boxcars away.

There had been three air strikes on Saint George's Day. On the twenty-fourth, there were so many that at noon a young American Air Force lieutenant who was serving as liaison between the brigade and its tactical air support stopped keeping track of individual strikes, as he had been conscientiously doing up to then. Probably some fifty planes gave the brigade a hand that morning. There were plenty of targets available to them. So many Chinese had infiltrated around the Glosters' flanks, both of which were by then exposed, that one air observer spotted some seven hundred of them standing around nonchalantly in a single group, in the open. One dive-bomber seared a Chinese-held hill with napalm. The nine Glosters captured the day before were on it, along with their guards. Several of the guards caught fire, and while they were frantically trying to beat out the flames, seven of the Glosters, who had somehow contrived to avoid being more than uncomfortably warmed, ran down the hill and escaped into the lines held by the Fusiliers and the Rifles. This was a particular relief to one of them, who had spent five years in a Nazi prisoner-of-war enclosure. The Fusiliers and the Rifles were better off than the Glosters, but they were having no picnic, either. There were Chinese behind them, too, and brigade headquarters organized a makeshift reinforcement party to help them out. It was composed of what little could then be mustered for the purpose: eight tanks from the Hussars, some Royal Engineers acting as infantry, a few Royal Army Service Corps lorries—which under normal circumstances wouldn't be sent too near the enemy but whose drivers in this instance volunteered to lumber along behind the tanks right to the front— and forty green replacements who had reported to the brigade that day and had been assigned to the Fusiliers. Some of them never got to report to the Fusiliers. There were so many enemy wandering around the countryside by then that the headquarters was under small-arms fire, and mortars were being lobbed out at the enemy from behind brigade headquarters—which, as a major in charge of the mortars later remarked, was a most ungentlemanly way to wage war.

The Glosters were in pretty bad shape on the morning of the twenty-fourth. The enemy had been at them all night long. Baker Company, which, like the three other rifle companies in the battalion, had a normal strength of a hundred and fifty men, was down to one officer and fifteen other ranks. It was nearly impossible to move out of a foxhole anywhere along the battalion line without drawing machine-gun fire. The Glosters nevertheless reassembled around a hill on which the battalion command post had been established. The line had shrunk from four miles to six hundred yards, but it still hadn't been breached. The Glosters begged several times that day for a helicopter to come and evacuate their more seriously wounded. The enemy, however, was so close on all sides that no helicopter could be sent out with any real hope of accomplishing this mission. That morning, Colonel Carne was asked if he thought a relief column could get through to him. He said no. (Communications with him had been spotty for some hours; artillery fire had knocked out all the telephone wires, and only two gradually fading radios linked the Glosters with the rest of the brigade.) That afternoon, in disregard of the Colonel's opinion, the first of three attempts to rescue the Glosters was made. A battalion of Filipino infantrymen and some supporting tanks got to within fifteen hundred yards of them, and then, in a defile, the lead tank was set afire, and the entire column was blocked and had to withdraw. Neither of the two subsequent relief columns—one composed of Belgian, Filipino, and

65

Puerto Rican infantrymen and elements of the 8th Hussars, and the other of tanks and infantrymen from the American 3rd Division—got even that close. When the third try had failed, the Glosters, by that time seven miles deep in Chinese, were on their own.

Early on the morning of the twenty-fifth, the brigade was finally instructed to pull back to new defensive positions. It had held up the Chinese long enough to disrupt their timetable all across the front. Those of the Fusiliers and Rifles who could walk managed to withdraw in fairly good order. The non-walking wounded from these units were worse off. Some two hundred of them were loaded onto the backs and sides of eight Centurions, which started off toward the rear through a narrow mountain pass. They were ambushed by the Chinese. The wounded, lying exposed on the tanks, couldn't do anything about it, and the tank crews were almost as impotent. Their vehicles were so slippery with blood and so jammed with sprawled bodies that it was impossible to traverse the gun turrets. On the way out, two tank commanders were wounded. Both remained standing in their hatchways, one fainting there and reassuming command when he came to. An officer riding on the outside of one Centurion, who while aboard ship en route to Korea the previous fall had entertained at a troop show by putting on a fake mental-telepathy act, was startled when one of the wounded men raised his head and said, "Beg pardon, sir, but there's something I've been wanting to ask you. How'd you do that bloody trick?" The driver of another Centurion, one that had no wounded on it and was, accordingly, buttoned up tight, was surprised to hear a thumping noise overhead. Looking up through his periscope, he saw a Chinese soldier perched above him, pounding on the hatch cover in an effort to open it. Without slowing down, the driver swerved to one side, drove the tank clean through a Korean house, brushing the interloper off, and then resumed his course.

Before daylight each morning during the battle, the Chinese had been sounding the bugle calls with which they customarily herald their armed approach. Before dawn on the twenty-fifth, the three hundred or so Glosters who were still fit to fight counterattacked in just about the only manner left to them: their bugler blew a long reveille. It rang out, clear and astonishing, and it was followed by a series of other calls—short reveille, half-hour dress, quarter-hour dress, cookhouse, and, just for the hell of it, the American variation of reveille. It was an amazing concert. For the few minutes it lasted, both sides stopped firing. Then the Glosters cheered, and the

67

fighting started up again. At five minutes past six, shortly after daybreak, the Glosters were advised by brigade headquarters that they had permission to break out. At six-twenty, the Glosters reported that they were surrounded and couldn't break out. But they still wanted air support, and they got it. By almost split-second co-ordination between air and artillery, a flight of dive-bombers swooped on the enemy just one and a half minutes after the artillery lifted a barrage it had been laying in. The Glosters by then were down to one small yellow air-ground recognition panel, and it was hard for the diving aircraft to know exactly where to strafe and bomb. But the Glosters threw a couple of smoke grenades out from their perimeter—thirty-five yards is a fair throw with a smoke grenade—and the planes aimed their machine guns where the grenades landed. Then bombs were dropped, at a somewhat, but not terribly much, more circumspect distance. The Chinese were hurt, and momentarily relaxed their pressure.

Colonel Carne summoned his company commanders to a hollow near his headquarters, where fifty or sixty stretcher cases were lying on the ground. He told them that all hope of carrying on as a unit was gone. He said he was going to stay where he was, and he gave them the option of surrendering or fighting

68

their way out in separate groups. The commanders of Able, Baker, and Charlie Companies and their remaining men headed south, toward the United Nations lines. It was the commander of Dog Company, Captain Mike Harvey, a twenty-eight-year-old officer from Portsmouth, who led out the group of thirty-nine that got back. He was in charge of Dog Company only by chance; its regular commander, a major, had gone to Japan on April 22nd for a rest. When the major arrived there, he heard that the spring offensive had started and caught the first plane back to Korea. Despite several tries, he was never able to make his way far enough forward to reach his unit. Harvey, a pink-cheeked man with horn-rimmed glasses and an unkempt mustache, is a Reserve officer who was in the Hampshire Regiment during the Second World War; up to April 22nd, he had thought of himself as a Hampshire man on loan to the Gloucestershire Regiment. Now he thinks of himself, without reservation, as a Gloster. He is unusually abstemious for a soldier, forgoing both tobacco and alcohol, principally because he has been interested in judo since the age of twelve and holds one of the highest ratings in the art. After he had assembled his withdrawal party, consisting then of twelve officers and ninety-two other ranks, he let the remnants of the three other companies start off ahead. "I stood on a hill watching them to see if they were really going," he said afterward. "It was unbelievable that things had come to this pass." He decided not to go south himself but instead to try the unexpected and proceed due north for a mile, straight toward the Chinese rear, and then swing west a couple of miles, in an outflanking movement, before turning south. He warned his group that they would have to travel fast, exhausted though they were, and that there could be no stopping to aid anybody who might be wounded.

Proceeding cautiously, Harvey and his men didn't see a single Chinese for the first three miles. His scheme was working fine. Then, just as they were veering south, they ran into a few Chinese. The Glosters shot them and moved on. When only a few miles from a point where they thought friendly troops would be, they were heartened by the appearance overhead of a Mosquito plane, generally used as liaison between ground forces and fighter aircraft. The Mosquito circled above them and wagged its wings encouragingly, and they waved back. The Mosquito began to guide them homeward through the hills. Harvey was keeping his men on low ground whenever possible, knowing that the Chinese habitually congregate on ridges. Ultimately, they came into one valley, two miles long, that was almost a canyon, with precipitous walls on both sides and a floor about a quarter-mile wide. A stream flowed through it, and they waded along this for a mile or so, until it dwindled away. As they came out on dry ground, thirty or forty machine guns opened up on them, from both flanks. The Glosters made for a ditch about a foot deep and dived into it. By then, the Mosquito had radioed for fighter planes, and they had come buzzing along and were working over the slopes as energetically as they could. But the machine guns didn't let up. The Glosters crawled forward, keeping their heads below the level of the ditch, since raising them as much as an inch above it had already proved fatal to several. The ditch, like the river bed before it, was full of stones, and the soldiers' arms and legs were lacerated. One man's shoes had fallen apart in the river, but he kept going, first in his socks and then, as those disintegrated, barefoot. Every so often, the men came to a four- or five-yard stretch where the ditch petered out, and in the stumbling race for the next ditch more were hit and dropped.

Finally, rounding a bend, they saw some American tanks down the valley, just half a mile away. They crawled ahead eagerly, and got to within five hundred yards of them. The tanks opened up with machine guns and 76-mm. cannon, and the six Glosters in the lead fell. The Mosquito pilot, horrified by this case of mistaken identity—the tank men had no idea any friendly troops were still that far north—flew frantically toward the tanks, diving almost on top of them, but they kept on firing. Harvey's single file of men, on their bellies in the ditch, were receiving fire from the front and both sides, and the men at the rear of the column, most of whom had exhausted their ammunition, were being stabbed by Chinese who had rushed down the valley behind them. Harvey tied his handkerchief and scarf to a stick, put his cap on it, and waved it at the tanks. Simultaneously, the Mosquito made another pass at the tanks and dropped them a note. The tanks, suddenly aware of their error, ceased firing. The remaining Glosters reached the tanks and crouched behind them. Using them as a partial shield against the continuing enemy fire, they withdrew another five hundred yards, to the reverse slope of a small hill. There they climbed on the tanks and rode out, for three more miles under steady enemy fire. The tank men were heartsick over their mistake. One of them took off his shoes and gave them to the Gloster who'd lost his. The lieutenant in command of the tanks kept asking how many of the Glosters his people had wounded. The Glosters, not wanting to make him feel any worse, wouldn't tell him; indeed, they didn't know for sure. The lieutenant was wounded himself getting them out.

As soon as Harvey got to a telephone, he called brigade headquarters. "I thought we had better get back, in case they wanted us again," he explained later. "Then I learned that we were the only survivors and that everyone else was missing." A week after the battle, the Glosters he had led out invited him to stop by for a beer. He hadn't touched the stuff in over three years, but to please them he drank a glass. "It tasted pretty awful," he said. "Being a judo man, it doesn't suit me."

The 1st Battalion of the Gloucestershire Regiment began reorganizing the day after the Battle of the Imjin ended. A few days after that, the handful of men from the old battalion and the new replacements lined up in a green Korean field for a simple memorial service. Massed around a table covered with a white cloth and bearing a cross and two candles, they stood with heads bared as their new battalion chaplain walked toward them in a white robe. Captain Harvey, now the battalion's new adjutant, distributed hymnals. The Glosters sang two hymns and, snapping to attention, a stanza of "God Save the King." After a few words from the battalion's new commander, who himself had been shot in the wrist during the Battle of the Imjin, the chaplain recited the names of the known dead, and the names of Colonel Carne and Sergeant Major Hobbs, as symbolic of, respectively, the officers and other ranks listed as missing. Then the chaplain told a story from Ecclesiastes about a city under siege, and how, after all hope was seemingly gone, a good and wise man had saved it. And yet, in spite of that, the chaplain said, the poor wise man was very soon forgotten. "In England, they'll remember for a little while," he went on. "The soldier does have his day. I want to remind you this afternoon that it is not enough to remember now. We've got to show what we think of their sacrifice in the way we conduct ourselves in the days ahead. We are, as it were, a link between our past and the future, and if we are to be faithful to our past, we must hand on to future generations some of the heritage of the past. Having handed it on, we will be in some measure worthy of those who died that we might live."

6

I FIRST met Sergeant First Class Joseph P. Reeves, a twenty-four-year-old soldier and the highest-ranking enlisted man of the second platoon of George Company of the 2nd Battalion of the 27th Infantry Regiment of the 25th Infantry Division—a celebrated regiment often known simply by its nickname, the Wolfhounds—on the morning of April 23rd, a few miles north of the Thirty-eighth Parallel. The Chinese had just begun their spring offensive, and I was waiting on the south bank of the Hantan River, together with some other correspondents, for a detail of engineers to demolish a long, dirt-topped bridge they had built across it only a couple of weeks earlier. The engineers, in turn, were waiting for a long column of troops and vehicles to withdraw over the bridge before blowing it up.

George Company of the 27th Infantry was one of the last units to come back across, and its men looked tired and dejected. Not only were they having to retrace their steps over ground they had such a short time before gone to considerable pains to occupy but they had had a protracted fire fight during the night. The second platoon, we'd heard, had acquitted itself more than handsomely. One of the other correspondents, having heard also that thirty out of the forty men in that platoon were replacements, was wondering how they had reacted as individuals to their initiation into battle. When the platoon came shuffling by, he asked its sergeant to stop for a moment. Reeves dropped out of line. He is a stocky, soft-speaking, open-faced man with a ruddy complexion. His clothes were dirty and he evidently hadn't shaved for a couple of days, but, considering the circumstances, he seemed unusually chipper, and he replied patiently and fully to the questions that were put to him. "The new men did pretty good, all in all," he said. "These Chinks were coming right in on us, but still my boys held their fire till they were only

76

thirty yards away. I was playing it cool. I was running up and down the line, talking them through it. A man who's not ever been in combat don't know how to act. An old man's got to drag him through it." A couple of minutes later, Reeves excused himself, so he could catch up with the platoon. I was impressed with his self-assurance and articulateness, and I hoped to run into him again somewhere.

It was less than a week later that I next heard of Sergeant Reeves. I was spending what I hoped would be a fairly quiet night at the headquarters of the 2nd Battalion of the 27th Infantry—the battalion of which George Company is a part—whose commanding officer, Lieutenant Colonel Richard Byrne, an Irishman from East Braintree, Massachusetts, flew a big green flag on his command jeep with "ERIN GO BRAUGH" lettered on it. (That was the way he chose to spell it, and, after all, it was his battalion.) Colonel Byrne's command post was set up in the principal room of a thatched Korean hut. It had a dirt floor about ten feet square, covered here and there with rice-straw matting, and it was furnished with a table, a chair, a map board, a naked light bulb, and several telephones. There was no bunting, aside from a blanket tacked over the outside door for blackout purposes. At five minutes after eight, Byrne was advised that bugles had been heard four hundred yards in front of George Company. Then came word that there were Chinese sharing some of George's foxholes, and then that one of George's platoons—not the second—had been overrun. Presently, Byrne was advising regimental headquarters, over one telephone, "They're pouring in by the thousands!" and Byrne's executive officer was simultaneously saying to a young field-artillery lieutenant attached to the command post, "Get that artillery out there on the double, by the battalion!" The lieutenant picked up another phone and shouted, "All right, let's go. Continuous firing. Everything you've got, just as fast as you can . . . You'd better get it out there, or they'll be shaking hands with you . . . Hell, I don't know how many's out there. What do you want me to do—count their dogtags?"

The rest of the night was anything but quiet, with Chinese roaming all over the battalion area, but even so there were lulls. During one of them, just after a runner had come in from up forward with a report on George Company's situation, Colonel Byrne, who was sitting on the floor with his back against a wall and the map board balanced on his raised knees, said to one of his staff officers, a captain who had once been in command of George Company, "Say, I

78

wonder how Reeves is doing tonight?" The captain was lying flat on his back, with his head under the table, his eyes closed, and a telephone instrument resting against each ear. Without opening his eyes, he began to chat with the Colonel about Reeves, and, among other things, they mentioned how, a few months back, the Sergeant had been just another inexperienced young infantryman—he enlisted in 1947—not noticeably more or less promising than any other, but how, like quite a few other American soldiers in Korea, he had evolved into a tough, skilled, professional fighting man. Byrne remarked that he hoped sooner or later to be able to get Reeves a battlefield commission, and somebody who was lying in a corner, apparently asleep, piped up, "I hear he was quite a hero the night the Chinaman started his big attack." The captain with the two telephones opened his eyes. "He's a hero every night," he said, and closed them again.

I decided to seek out Reeves, and several days later, when the action had let up somewhat and the battalion was dug in snugly behind the Seoul defense line, I spent a couple of hours talking with him, as the two of us sprawled comfortably on a dike in a paddy field, under a warm spring sun. I asked him first how his platoon had made out that night I had

79

been at battalion headquarters, and he said fine, although there had been a few tense moments when the Chinese outflanked them. "Hell, we wouldn't have had anything to worry about, even with all those Chinks around, if somebody in that other platoon hadn't hollered 'Move out!'" he said. "That left a big hole in the line. These people have got to learn you can't just take off like that. If you do that sort of thing, you're not handling your men whatsogoddamever."

Sergeant Reeves, I soon gathered, had given a lot of thought to the handling of men. He himself, of course, was subordinate to his platoon leader, a lieutenant named James A. Parker, for whom he had vast respect and admiration and who had spent nine months on combat duty in a rifle platoon, but he was acutely conscious of his responsibilities as Parker's deputy and as the chief noncommissioned officer of the platoon. "When you get into a position like mine," he told me, "you're not supposed to be up where the fighting is. You're supposed to run things from the rear. You're a little general." Except perhaps among the members of rifle squads, who in battle are apt to be all of thirty or forty yards forward of their platoon command post, a job such as Reeves has is not widely considered a sinecure, but he wasn't kidding when

80

he referred to the "rear"; he thinks of his squad leaders as the real front-line commanders.

Since October, 1950, when the little general first saw Korea, he had earned three Purple Hearts, a Silver Star, and a Bronze Star Medal—an estimable but not a terribly unusual record for a rifle-company noncom who had been around and alive that long— and he told me that he would like also to earn a Distinguished Service Cross, which is given, except sometimes in the cases of big generals, only for extraordinary heroism. "I've worked awfully hard trying to get that thing," Reeves said. (I was glad to hear a few weeks afterward that he had just been awarded the D.S.C.) Variously employing an M-1 rifle, a carbine, and his favorite weapon, the hand grenade, he had personally accounted for, by his own reckoning, more than two hundred enemy dead, or the equivalent of five platoons. He prefers the M-1 to the carbine. "The carbine fires too fast," he told me. "It'll get off thirty rounds before you know it. When a man is shooting at somebody—I don't care who he is—he gets excited and grabs that trigger, and if he's got a carbine, his weapon will just keep on talking. That's wasteful. Hell, you can kill a man with one or two rounds as easy as with thirty." Sergeant Reeves always carries an extra-sharp bayonet with him, too, but although his contact with the Chinese has been exceedingly intimate, he doubted whether he had ever killed one of them with it. "I've stuck a couple after I got 'em down," he said, "but I think they were dead already."

Like so many other men who enlisted in the Regular Army during peacetime, Sergeant Reeves is a Southerner. He was born on June 7, 1926, in Tallahassee, Florida, which has been his home all his life except for a couple of years in the thirties, when his father, a building contractor, was working in Texas. The Sergeant is the oldest of seven children. He has two brothers, both of whom have also served in the armed forces. In the spring of 1943, just as he was finishing his second year at Leon County High, in Tallahassee, he decided to give up school and join the Navy. "We were living on a little country farm outside Tallahassee then," he said, "and all the boys I'd been running round the woods with were being drafted, so I thought what the hell!" His parents were unenthusiastic about his notion but finally gave him permission to enlist. (In 1948, not long after joining the Army, he took some correspondence courses and received a high-school diploma.) He went through boot camp at Bainbridge, Maryland, and then was assigned to a vessel that ferried cargo and personnel around the Pacific bases. He stayed with it for thirteen months. "Then I got tired of the water and put in for a transfer," he said. "They gave me my choice of submarines or naval air. I was in Hawaii at the time, and I spent three and a half days sitting on the bottom in a sub and then I said, 'I'll take upstairs. If anything happens there, I might be able to come down, but if anything happens down below, I don't know that I can get up.'" The Navy obligingly put him through a brief course of air training, and then made him flight engineer aboard an air freighter that was based at Saipan. During the nine months he remained in its crew, it touched down at just about every big Pacific port. Once, in the summer of 1945, crippled by engine trouble, it also touched down in open water a hundred and seventy miles from the nearest land, Eniwetok. Reeves and his ten fellow-crewmen were picked up by a cutter after spending two and a half days in a rubber lifeboat.

Soon after that, Reeves's hitch expired and he was discharged. Returning to Tallahassee, he went into his father's contracting business, and by 1947 had worked his way up to the job of carpenter foreman. "Then, one morning," he told me, "I climbed down off a roof I was working on and left the ladder leaning against it and said, 'The hell with it! I'm going into the Army.' I just got itchy feet again, I guess. I gave up a dollar-seventy-five an hour. I could have kicked myself a million times since I done it. Even so, after I'd served my eighteen months, I re-enlisted. Don't ask me why." Reeves, who as a sergeant first class now earns, including allowances, two hundred a month, took his basic training in infantry, part of it at Fort Jackson, South Carolina, and the remainder at Fort McClellan, Alabama, where he lost two front teeth as a lightweight on the boxing team. Then the Army, in its mysterious way, shipped him to Fort Sam Houston, Texas, and he found himself in the medics, handling linen supply. He did that for a year and achieved the rating of corporal. "Pretty soon I wised off to a sergeant, with twenty-seven years in, about whether I should wear whites or fatigues while sandpapering some damned bedside tables," he said. "After the sergeant's colonel had busted me, I was offered a choice of going into the kitchen or cutting grass and such—you know, being an all-around yard-bird. I took the kitchen." Presently, following a spell at a cooks-and-bakers school, he became a full-fledged cook in the hospital kitchen, in charge of special diets. "There were four hundred and ten of those diets," he told me. "I didn't think there were so many different ways a person had to eat." While assigned

84

to the hospital, Reeves, who had made corporal again, met a Wac from the Bronx who was also stationed there. She is now out of the Army and taking a nurses'-training course in Mount Vernon, in Westchester, and he expects to marry her. "We're supposed to be officially engaged," he said, "but I haven't given her a ring yet, because she won't accept one by mail."

In September, 1950, Reeves embarked for Korea, still as a cook for the medics. He disembarked at Pusan. He had no particular feelings then about the United Nations or the political status of Korea, nor did he acquire any in the ensuing months; his feeling was that he was just a soldier doing his job wherever the Army elected to have him do it. By the time he got to Korea, he had become adept not only at preparing many dishes but, in the traditional manner of Army cooks, at sampling nearly all he prepared. From his boxing weight of a hundred and thirty, he had ballooned up to two hundred and twelve. "I couldn't put a khaki shirt on," he told me. "I didn't have no neck. That's the advantage of being a cook. But not long after I got to Korea, I went down like the price of good whiskey went up." (Reeves had last tasted whiskey two and a half months before our talk, when, thanks to an enterprising supply officer, each squad of George Company got a fifth of it, to be divided among the squad's nine members.) His reducing was accelerated by his having to go on a special diet himself—a soup one. This became obligatory when, shortly after he reached Korea, a truck he was riding in came under a North Korean mortar barrage, swerved to one side, and ran into another truck. Both Reeves's jaws were fractured. He was evacuated to a hospital in Yokohama, where he stayed until mid-November, with his jaws wired together.

The day after Reeves was unwired, he was sent back to Korea. There was an acute shortage of trained infantrymen, and since Reeves had taken basic training in that branch of the service, he was ordered to the 25th Division as a replacement, and landed in George of the 27th. "I felt kind of good, because I thought maybe I'd end up in the company kitchen," he said. "But when I got to George, I found the kitchen was filled up, and they put me in the second platoon, on top of one of the highest goddam hills in Korea. That was on November 28th, the day after the first big bugout to the south started. I still had my corporal's rating. They asked me if I'd ever handled men, and I said 'Yeah,' and they asked me if I thought I'd like to be an assistant squad leader, and I said 'Give me a shot at it.' They introduced me to

86

the other guys in the platoon and said this one
had been put in for Silver Star this, and that one had
been put in for Silver Star that, and I looked at
them and thought, They ain't done a goddam thing
I can't do. Three weeks later, my squad leader froze
his feet, and I took over.

"I had a pretty good poker hand," Reeves continued. "Five deuces. Second squad of the second
platoon of the Second Battalion of the Two-seven
Regiment of the Two-five Division. And a funny thing
was that the first time I ran into any Chinks—it was
at exactly fifteen minutes to four on the morning
of January 4th—I had two tanks with my squad. Our
job was to block a road that George Company was
pulling out on. We were supposed to hold for two
hours, till daylight, and we did. There wasn't anything a *bit* funny about its being two hours, because
that was in the middle of winter and we were freez-
ing to death standing there. Well, everything was
peaceful enough until around a bend came some
Chinks, talking to each other just like they were on
a moonlight walk or something, and one of them
riding a bicycle. I was set to ambush them when a
damn fool of a South Korean soldier who was with
me stepped out and hailed them and started a conversation. Then he hollered 'Enemy!' and everybody

87

started shooting. My hands were so goddam cold I couldn't hardly load my rifle, but after a couple of clips had gone through it, I started sweating, what with those Chink bullets dancing off our tanks like somebody was throwing rice. That was my first real infantry battle."

Eleven days after that encounter, on another cold night, Reeves and some other men lit a bonfire to warm themselves. He wasn't sure precisely what happened—he thought they might have laid the fire on top of a small mine—but in any event there was an explosion, and he was evacuated to a hospital in Taegu, with shrapnel in both thighs, one eye, and his chin. None of the wounds was serious, and he returned to duty in a week.

For three months from the end of January on, almost without interruption, Sergeant Reeves had been leading the life of an infantryman in battle. On the surface, at least, it seemed to have agreed with him. His weight was down to about a hundred and forty-five, and he had a perfectly discernible neck. He had seen so much action that he could recall only the highlights of it, and in discussing them he sounded a trifle didactic. It was as if he had discussed them several times before, perhaps in the course of teaching young-puppy riflemen his old-dog tricks.

"The hardest thing for me is getting started," he said. "I'm always thinking, If they get me in the arm or the leg, I'll get out all right, but what if they get me in the head? I'm always sweating out my head. There was this time there were these three machine guns on a hillside, pinning the whole platoon down, and the order came 'Take that goddam hill'—that's just the way it came. I had charge of two squads then, and I got them together and I says, 'The Old Man says, "Take that hill." We got to go, men.' They said, 'Yep, somebody's got to go.' Nobody made a move, so I finally says, 'All right, by the help of God and my M-1 rifle, we're going to take that hill.' I sling my M-1 around my neck and take a grenade in each hand and start off, and I drop one grenade in one machine-gun hole and the other in another, and my men took care of the third gun. We got twenty-six Chinks, and only one casualty of our own. He was shot through the chest—left side, too—but he lived. I got a letter from the old boy the other day. From Hawaii. He got that million-dollar wound.

"That action was in February," Reeves went on, "and there were a couple of beauties in March. But in April, when we got north of the Parallel again, things really got interesting. I made platoon sergeant the fourth of the month, and a couple of weeks after, we came to a hill called Jake Able. Easy and Fox Companies were run off the hill, and Battalion ordered George to take it back. Three squads of my platoon were leading. The first two got pinned down, and then the third took off and worked to the top of the hill and got itself into a stiff fire fight. I was back where the platoon sergeant is supposed to be, on the radio, but I couldn't stay there any longer. I threw my damn radio down and I took off. Well, the way Jake Able was, the Chinks had it dug in real good, with four machine-gun nests on it. I told my men to give me some covering fire, and I grab a box of grenades. 'You're going to get killed,' a guy told me. Well, I get up in a bunch of these *mak* trees and Joe Chink throws a grenade at me. I can't move without exposing myself, so I reach down to pick it up and throw it back, and just as I throw it, it goes off. It turned me over and knocked me fruitier than a nut-cake. Then I got hot under the collar. I called for a flamethrower, and with that, and my grenades, I got a lot of them, six in one hole, two in another—I don't know how many altogether. After all the fireworks stopped, I'm sitting there shaking, waiting for Lieutenant Parker to chew me for being in the wrong place. But he said, 'I'm not going to chew you. I want to shake your hand.' I had to shake with my left hand,

90

because my right was all bruised and swole up from the grenade. But, be that as it may, I probably still shouldn't have been where I was. Then, in mid-April, rotation started, and these replacements came in—the sorriest bunch you ever saw. They're overweight, they can't walk, they can't do this, they can't do that. If they'd get rid of those goddam classrooms in the States and start 'em marching and tearing down machine guns and rifles, you'd have some soldiers. When my new men came in, at first I more or less had to use the Patton way on them—get behind 'em and drive 'em, talk 'em through it, keep 'em cooled down. This night before we came back over the Hantan, for instance, the Lieutenant was sleeping and I was manning the platoon telephone when the bugles and green flares began. I hadn't been able to sleep at all—I'd had a funny feeling in my neck. When I saw the flares, I hollered that the Chinks were on the way. Then they threw a five-minute barrage of artillery on us—every goddam thing under the sun. Then came their infantry, one wave after another. I move around among my men, hollering like a Comanche or something, 'Hold your fire till they get close! Hold your fire till they get close enough to smell their breath!' One of the new men yelled back, 'They're spitting on me now! All right to shoot?,' so I figured he'd turned out O.K. You know, handling forty men really keeps you busy. For a country boy, that's pretty stiff work. When it got daylight, and I found out we didn't have a single casualty, I think I was about the happiest man who ever did have a platoon."

Sergeant Reeves said he'd have to leave in a couple of minutes to check some defensive positions his men were supposed to be improving. I asked him what he thought his chances were of being rotated. He said he had no idea; all he knew was that he was already eligible. Regardless of whether he was kept in Korea for a while—and, owing to a shortage of knowledgeable noncoms of his type, it was conceivable that he might be, eligibility or no eligibility—or was stationed somewhere else, he still had a year to go on his present enlistment. He didn't know what he wanted to do after that. "I like the Army," he said. "The Army's been good to me. I wouldn't mind staying in—I could retire at thirty-seven, counting in my Navy time and everything—but I don't know. I want to get married and get me a home and a couple of kids—something I can really call my own. I never had nothing I could really call my own except a Ford, and I sold that. I want something that I can say, 'Well, that's mine.' If I got a job in the States training troops somewhere, I could get me a car, and

92

maybe that wouldn't be too bad. But I don't like it here. I can't take too much more of this. I've been to Hong Kong and Shanghai, and still I never saw so goddam many Chinamen. I don't underestimate these Chinks. They're Chinese and they're enemy, but they're good soldiers. They're not *better* soldiers —I'll outsoldier and outshoot any of 'em—but they're good. Before I came over here, I thought these Chinks and North Koreans, they was crazy as hell— a bunch of gooks jumping the American Army after we'd just whipped the Japs and Germans. All I can say now is 'Kill them before they kill you.' To put it in one of my pet country expressions, it's 'Root, hog—or die poor,' and I intend to die fat. There aren't enough Chinks in China to kill me. I got too much to look forward to."

7

SIXTY miles south of the Korean Peninsula lies the island province of Cheju-do, which is regarded by the mainlanders—not to mention those Americans who have seen enough of the Peninsula for its peculiarities not to seem conspicuous to them any more—as a mighty quaint spot. Cheju-do, which is some fifty miles long and averages fifteen miles in width, and has a normal peacetime population of about two hundred and fifty thousand, is, among other odd things, one of the world's foremost citadels of matriarchy. Its native women outnumber its native men three to one, and not only do they enjoy statis-

94

tical superiority but they have taken over many of the characteristics and duties of the conventionally stronger sex. Male residents of Cheju-do have been known to quail at a brandished female fist, and not without reason, for the women of Cheju-do are formidably built and remarkably sturdy. They plow the fields, operate the fishing boats, look after the livestock, and tote the heavy loads. On the Korean Peninsula, women customarily balance their burdens on their heads, while men carry theirs—usually weightier ones—on A-frames. On Cheju-do, women use A-frames, too. In some of the villages, where newfangled ideas of sex equality have not yet crept in, the men cook, keep house, and tend the children who are past nursing age. While I was there on a visit, I noticed several women wrestling unruly horses into submission; nearby stood some men clutching the hands of small children, who are no more unruly on Cheju-do than in Westchester County.

Korea is full of legends, and a popular one in explanation of the preponderance of women on Cheju-do has it that many years ago the adults of the island were exclusively female. Once a year, the story goes, a batch of men were ferried over from the mainland and, after a brief rendezvous with the local population, were whisked away again. The sons resulting from this annual dalliance were exiled, too, as soon as they had been weaned. However that may be, for quite some time now, males have been permitted to be year-round residents of the island, and on occasion even to take what is elsewhere generally recognized as their place, but they have not yet caught up with the ladies. Their chances of doing so in the immediate future seem slim, for many of Cheju-do's men, like those from all the rest of Korea, have gone into the armed forces, and several thousand others have died in the guerrilla fighting that has been an intermittent feature of the island's community life since 1947. The island's womenfolk have let the men have these skirmishes pretty much to themselves, perhaps having decided cagily at the outset that any casualties they themselves might suffer would endanger their pre-eminence.

By what seems an almost incredible coincidence, this Amazonish island has on it a special group of strong-armed women called *amah sans*—a term of Japanese origin meaning "sea girls." They are exceptional swimmers, and even in the wintertime can be found off-shore, diving for the petrified remains of submerged pine trees and for abalones, pearls, and seaweed, a popular food hereabouts. As implements of their trade, the *amah sans* employ straw baskets and hollow gourds that help support them as they paddle out to work. When they dive, they leave this equipment floating on the surface; when they come up, they stuff whatever they have harvested into their receptacles, which they tow ashore when they are ready to call it a day. Nobody I talked to in Korea knew whether or not any etymological-minded anthropologist had ever attempted to establish a connection between the *amah sans* and the Amazons of Greek mythology, or, for that matter, between them and the Amazon River.

It has been fairly well established, though, that the people of Cheju-do are a mixture of several scattered bloodlines. The island is a halfway point between Japan and China, and for hundreds of years it has been a stopping-off place for merchant vessels. Sailors have settled there whose ports of origin were, among other places, the Philippines, Borneo, Malaya, Holland, and Spain, as well as the part of northern Japan occupied by aborigines called Ainus, who, as far as I know, have otherwise migrated merely to crossword puzzles. The inhabitants of Cheju-do, however, are thought to be primarily descended from some Mongolians who appeared on Cheju-do in the thirteenth century, shortly after Genghis Khan invaded and took over the Korean

97

mainland. Many of the islanders have Mongolian features. The island abounds with cattle (Genghis Khan and his men were great ones for livestock) and with small, shaggy horses, both wild and tame, that could pass for Mongolian ponies anywhere. As mementos of bygone voyagers from more southerly areas, Cheju-do has a number of coconut groves and what its governor proudly assured me is the only banana tree in all Korea.

Even those residents of Cheju-do who will unhesitatingly admit to a Mongolian gene or two in their makeup insist loyally on giving the main credit for their origin—and, in fact, for the origin of the whole Korean race—to a snow-capped volcanic mountain called Halla-san, which rises to a height of close to seven thousand feet in the center of the island. The story is that somewhere between four and five thousand years ago Halla-san propelled from its crater three men, named Ko, Pu, and Yang, who were the very first Koreans. They came to earth seven or eight miles from the peak of the mountain, near what is now the city of Cheju, on the northern coast. I was taken to a carefully tended shrine on the outskirts of Cheju where, in a fenced-off circular area about thirty feet in diameter, there are three dents in the ground, resembling shallow foxholes. These are said to be the landing places of Ko, Pu, and Yang. How these gentlemen discovered any ladies with whom to get the next generation of Koreans started—or why so markedly feministic an island has so long cherished such a masculine theory of evolution—is something that none of the islanders I asked about it could explain.

There is no doubt that Halla-san, though now extinct, was, in its day, a prodigiously explosive mountain. All the way to its coasts, Cheju-do is littered with hunks of volcanic rock. The countryside bristles with stone walls, and practically all the houses on the island, which with few exceptions are close to the sea, have been built—in many cases by lady masons —out of stone. (On the Peninsula, the chief building material is dirt.) As in Korea proper, most of the Cheju-do houses have thatched roofs, but on the island the roofs are lashed down with crisscrossed ropes, which are moored to the rafters and look like giant hair nets. These do not represent the womanly touch but are inspired by Cheju-do's winds, which are brisk. (The place is sometimes called "the island of wind, women, and stones.") The villages, except where they are bounded by the sea, are encircled by stone walls seven or eight feet high. There is only one road suitable for vehicular traffic—a dirt-and-stone

99

affair, slightly more than a hundred miles long, that follows the coastline all the way around the island. Wherever the road passes through a village, the ends of the wall surrounding the community extend right to the edge of the driving surface on either side of the right of way and have gates attached to them. At night, these gates are closed and bolted across the road. It is possible to travel around Cheju-do after dark only by notifying the village police in advance. Otherwise, the gates stay shut until dawn.

Few residents of the island felt disposed to wander about after dark anyway, when I was there. One reason for this cautious attitude in a province safely remote from its country's battlefields was the presence in the foothills of Halla-san of small but irritating bands of native pro-Communist guerrillas. Four years earlier, some ten thousand guerrillas had been active there, and it had required a prolonged effort on the part of the South Korean Constabulary— the forerunners of the present Republic of Korea Army—to flush the bulk of them out. (One of the Army's officers told me that prior to this island conflict there were more than a hundred thousand horses on Cheju-do, and by 1950 only twenty thousand; the guerrillas, he said, had eaten a good many of the missing ones.) Although Cheju-do has had a relatively peaceful time of it since 1949, some of the guerrillas managed to elude the constabulary and were still eluding the local police, whose responsibility they had become considered. Only a week before my visit, the governor of the island had appealed to the Army to do something about getting rid of them once and for all. The exact number of guerrillas still functioning was uncertain, but it was thought unlikely that the total was over a hundred. Even so, nobody from the coast felt terribly inclined to go up into the hills in search of them, and the centrally situated hiding places of the guerrillas made any village on the whole periphery of the island a potential target for a raid.

Forty-eight hours before my visit to Cheju-do, there had been one such raid. The soldiers in a Korean Army camp two miles from the scene hadn't even heard about it until the day of my arrival, for Korean civilians often don't bother to pass along information of this sort, not being aware that anybody would be especially interested in it. Inasmuch as Cheju-do is a mere two hundred and fifty miles by sea from Shanghai, this lack of communicativeness made some of the more sensitive United Nations people stationed on the island a bit apprehensive. "Someday," one American there remarked to me, "I expect

101

to have an *amah san* come up to me and say casually, 'Oh, I forgot to tell you that last Friday a hundred thousand Chinese Communists made a landing twenty miles up the coast.'" The usefulness of Cheju-do as a military outpost had already been demonstrated by the Japanese, who dispatched bombers from there to China before and during the Second World War, and at one time had two hundred thousand ground troops in training on it. The Japanese built airfields with underground concrete hangars and dug ammunition dumps in the sides of hills. (Cheju-do is currently noted in these parts for its cigarette holders, which the islanders make out of petrified wood, adding brass mouthpieces cut from old Japanese cartridge cases.)

At the time I was there, Cheju-do was serving as a sanctuary for sixty thousand refugees from the mainland and as a base for both the ROK, or Republic of Korea, Air Force and the ROK Army. The principal Army installation, which was set up where it was when the war was going badly during the winter and it seemed possible that the Eighth Army would have to quit the mainland, occupied the site of a former Japanese military camp and was a training center for Korean recruits. The Koreans, who are fond of decorative effects in and out of doors, had prettied

102

it up, to what may or may not have been good military purpose, with ornamental shrubbery, paths edged by white sea shells, colored gateways festooned with dragons and tigers, and innumerable stone walls— these last, naturally, constructed by women. The center could accommodate fourteen thousand recruits, part of whose education consisted of viewing United States Army training films with Korean sound tracks. (What I took to be the American influence was also evident in the form of signs in English reading, "Kim Il Sung is on the run" and "The hammer and sickle are in a pickle.") The center had all the usual facilities of its counterparts in the United States: rifle, automatic-rifle, machine-gun, carbine, and grenade ranges; bayonet, obstacle, and infiltration courses; and a PX, at which the wares on display included rice balls, cider, and dried fish. The soldiers sat in Buddha-like postures while receiving instruction, but when on the march resolutely shouted, "Hup, two, three, four" —in Korean, of course. The recruits slept in communal beds—a dozen of them to a raised platform, on which each had his assigned spot and his assigned blanket —and bathed in communal tubs, which are large tanks that will hold around twenty men at a splash. A drivers' school was to open the following week, which news I was certain would elate a good many

Americans on the mainland who felt, not entirely without justification, that their lives had occasionally been imperiled on the roads by the unfamiliarity of most Koreans with mechanized vehicles. The school was to have got under way sooner, but of thirty-eight Korean soldiers assigned to it as instructors, only five, it was discovered, knew how to drive an automobile.

While I was at the center, a visiting ROK general, exhorting a massed outdoor formation of recruits with the aid of a loudspeaker, mentioned the long and troubled history of Korea, which over the centuries has been occupied by Mongolians, Russians, Japanese, and Chinese. "The last four thousand two hundred and eighty years have been bad history for us," he told them, according to the interpreter who gave me a running translation of his remarks. "It's going to be up to you men to make new and better history." Some Cheju-do women hauling a load of stones along a nearby road were also listening, and, Oriental inscrutability notwithstanding, I was sure I saw a look of dismay cross their faces.

8

In its earliest days, the war in Korea was, at least on the firing line, a purely civil one between South and North Koreans. It was, of course, to become a far more complicated affair, but the easternmost part of the front, despite the internationalization of the rest of the battlefield, remained pretty much the scene of an exclusively civil war. In the middle of May, some Chinese turned up in the area, but this appears to have been mainly because they bounced off in that direction after bumping painfully into the United States 2nd Infantry Division during the second phase of the Communist spring offensive. Aside from these probably accidental incursions, the ground troops facing each other on the east were unexceptionally Korean, and their rivalry was often, by Occidental standards, rather bizarre. It was not unusual, for instance, for commanders of both North and South Korean forces to offer or concede prizes for objectives especially coveted or attained. After one ROK outfit had trounced a North Korean outfit in a certain engagement, every officer on the winning team was granted a month's extra pay and every enlisted man a promotion, with the result that the regiment found itself without a single private. Bonuses of five hundred thousand *won*—the rate of exchange was six thousand *won* to the dollar—were promised the ROKs for the capture of some particularly desirable enemy division commander, and of a hundred thousand *won* for any old enemy tank. Moreover, it was learned from prisoners that the North Koreans stood similarly ready to present the captor of any member of a notably efficient ROK reconnaissance company with three hundred thousand *won*. An American officer attached to the ROKs as an adviser was gratified to hear that his species had been singled out for special appraisal, too; the enemy rated him a fifty-thousand-*won*, or eight-dollar, trophy.

I visited the ROK forces in the east early in June,

106

at which moment they had pushed to some thirty miles north of the Thirty-eighth Parallel, which was then twenty miles forward of the line in any other sector and represented the northernmost advance made by any United Nations element since General MacArthur had tossed his boomerang at the Yalu River the previous fall. By and large, the operations on the east coast, most of them confined to the much-trodden zone just north of the Parallel, were conducted on a more modest scale than those elsewhere, seldom involving more than a battalion or two from each side at a time. For the government of South Korea, however, the events in that sector had considerable significance, for it was the only one in which the ROKs operated for any protracted stretch more or less on their own. All the South Koreans in action in other parts of the peninsula were under American corps; on the east, the ROK divisions were under a ROK corps, led by Major General Paik Sun Yup, the highest-ranking South Korean field commander, who was subsequently chosen as one of the United Nations delegates to the Kaesong talks. (That he happens to be a native of Pyongyang, the North Korean capital, was a circumstance no more confusing than many another of the war.)

On several occasions during the war, ROK units

showed themselves to be somewhat less resolute in holding positions than many of the transient defenders of their national sovereignty, and these lapses gave rise to a fair amount of skepticism about their basic capabilities as soldiers. The view held by numerous Americans that practically all ROKs were martially incompetent was decidedly antithetical to that held by, among others, President Syngman Rhee, who declared on one occasion that his citizens, if adequately trained, armed, and equipped, would be quite willing and able to take over the entire military campaign by themselves. The President's understandably chauvinistic opinion was echoed by the chief of staff of his Army, Lieutenant General Chung Il Kwon, who pointed out that whenever the Communists launched a big attack, they would go out of their way to strike hardest at ROK units, knowing that these were apt to have much less firepower than the units on their flanks. "To strengthen the ROK Army will be to destroy the enemy," General Chung said. Many Americans anxious to emigrate from the peninsula and not too passionately concerned about who relieved them would have been delighted if the ROK Army had been able to take over, but the ROK Army was, unfortunately, an awfully young and inexperienced organization. When

108

the North Koreans invaded South Korea, the ninety-six thousand ROK soldiers who opposed them were so far from being fully trained that none had ever taken part in any military maneuver more elaborate than a battalion exercise. In a month, fifty thousand of the ninety-six thousand had become casualties, and because of the exigencies of the situation at that time, they had had to be replaced by men only four or five days removed from civilian life. After nearly a year of fighting, the ROKs had suffered almost a hundred and forty thousand casualties—or half again as many soldiers as they had to begin with. Nonetheless, they had managed to piece together an army more than two hundred and fifty thousand strong. Some of these men had had the unique experience of fighting on both sides, having been captured by the North Koreans and impressed into their rifle squads (the North Koreans had special detachments of M.P.s charged with keeping prisoners there), and then, after escaping or being recaptured, having rejoined their original units.

The South Koreans had no great trouble recruiting manpower, since that was one of their few remaining assets, but they were seriously handicapped by a lack of qualified junior officers and noncommissioned officers. ROK soldiers appear to respond well to good leadership; one company, assaulted by a North Korean battalion while out in an exposed position, was inspired by its commander not only to beat off the enemy but to pursue it spiritedly. Good leadership, however, was rare enough to be considered noteworthy. One reason was the absence of any military tradition in Korea. During the years of Japanese occupation, rank-and-file Koreans were forbidden to use firearms even for hunting. The tools of war are still comparatively unfamiliar to most of them, for after the Japanese were evicted, the South Koreans were introduced to these gadgets by their American occupiers in a much more casual manner than were the North Koreans by their Soviet occupiers. Nearly all the general officers of the ROK Army are alumni of a select group of Koreans who were permitted by their penultimate overlords to join the Japanese Army (Japanese Army ways still persist in the ROK; its officers of the day customarily observe the Japanese practice of sporting gay red-and-white striped sashes), and they are far more youthful than the generals of other nations. General Chung, the chief of staff and an honor graduate of the Japanese Military Academy, is thirty-four. General Paik, the corps commander, is thirty and also a Japanese veteran. In 1946, he was a captain in the South Korean

Constabulary. The brigadier generals commanding the divisions in his corps were then all platoon commanders serving under him. Paik has a younger brother who is a ROK brigadier; when the latter was recommended for promotion to that grade, the elder Paik argued against it at first, on the ground that his brother, however deserving, was only twenty-seven and too young for such high rank.

By June, 1951, the ROK Army consisted of ten divisions, all of them numbered except the Capital Division, which acquired its name because it was stationed at Seoul when the war started and which, after withdrawing to the Pusan perimeter, became the mainstay of the ROK forces on the east coast. (There is no 4th Division; not only is the number regarded as unlucky in Korea, but a regiment with that designation gave an extremely shabby account of itself while attempting to subdue an uprising against the South Korean government in 1949, and ever since then the Republic's military men have avoided the use of that tarnished numeral at any unit level.) The ROK divisions differ markedly from their American counterparts. An American infantry division at authorized strength has about eighteen thousand men, a ROK division slightly under twelve thousand. An American division has four battalions of artillery, a

ROK division just one—and not because of a super-stitious reluctance to have three more but simply because no more are available. An American division has its own battalion of tanks, a ROK division has none at all. The same disparity exists in transporta-tion, communications, tactical air-liaison teams, and so on. In sum, the combat potential of a ROK divi-sion is about equal to that of an American regiment, or roughly one-third that of an American division.

The South Korean soldier is issued just one uni-form, and if he loses part of it, he is hard put to it to find a substitute. At the time of my trip to the east coast, the Capital Division was making gleeful use of a thousand blankets and three hundred pairs of shoes that it had captured from the enemy and pressed into immediate service. The east-coast terrain is even more mountainous than the rest of Korea, and the ROKs, for want of transport, generally move about on foot, but nevertheless most of the South Korean infantrymen there were outfitted not with leather boots but with sneakers, the soles of which wore through in about ten days of average activity. One ROK company commander told me that although he had often requested that all his hundred and fifty men be issued boots, just ten of them had any, and those only because they bought them on their own

112

hook in a public market, paying from thirty to forty thousand *won* a pair. This amounted to a mere five or six dollars, but it represented an enormous investment for a South Korean soldier, inasmuch as a private is paid three thousand *won* a month and even a brigadier general gets along on sixty thousand. The ROK Army is not the most amply fed in the world—or even, for that matter, in Korea—but its soldiers do get three servings of rice a day, and their units are also allotted a hundred *won* per man per day for the purchase of such supplementary foods as fish, seaweed, and vegetables. (Some soldiers fortified this ration by fishing in streams with hand grenades.) Field kitchens would normally consist of two or three large iron pots, set over an open fire. The ROKs had a C ration of their own; developed for them by the Eighth Army, it was packed in Japan and contained such fare as rice, starch, red pepper, green tea, dried codfish, dried cuttlefish, and kelp.

A feature of the operations of the ROK corps was its reliance on warships of the United Nations naval forces to provide supporting fire. (The South Korean Navy consisted solely of small patrol craft.) For months on end, these warships served as the ROKs' heavy artillery. The fleet on hand at any given time varied in number from three to five ships, in size from destroyers to battleships, in effective range from fifteen to twenty-five thousand yards, and in ports of origin from the United States to half a dozen other allied nations. Cruising up and down the coast—which, incidentally, has lovely white-sand beaches and in any more accessible part of the world would surely have long ago been decked out with resort hotels—the Navy, at the bidding of two American shore-control parties attached to the corps, would send a steady and comforting spray of steel over the heads of the South Koreans and into the North Koreans' positions. (Navy planes from nearby carriers also aided the ROKs by bombing and strafing the North Koreans.) Army officers ashore came to regard one destroyer as the equivalent in firepower of a battery of 155-mm. guns. A naval gunnery officer I talked to aboard one of the supporting vessels declined to estimate its worth in such prosaic, earthbound terms, but he did say cheerfully, "We're just a big seagoing artillery weapon." As such, the Navy has certain advantages over the conventional battery. It is more mobile, it can easily carry several hundred tons of ammunition around with it wherever it goes, it has much better range computers than land-based artillery, it can furnish its observers with more powerful optical equipment, it is in a better position to

114

keep its weapons in order, it can sail up behind the enemy lines and shell him from the rear, and it can provide its men with practically unlimited quantities of ice cream.

Largely because of the formidable presence of the Navy, the North Koreans shied away from spending any lengthy periods in the coastal fishing villages north of the Parallel, most of which had been demolished by one seagoing artillery weapon or another. The enemy stuck mostly to the mountains, which rise up sharply a few miles inland, in an attempt to stay out of range. Even if the South Koreans had had all the field artillery they wanted—and there has never been an infantryman of any race who thought he had enough—they'd have a hard time moving it about, for there are exceedingly few roads leading west from the coast anywhere near the Parallel. Troops had to rely on narrow mountain trails that curl along the high ridges and dip steeply between the hills. Some of the highest of these hills were still snow-covered on the eve of summer, but the majority of them were green with late-spring shrubbery and dotted with magnolia blossoms, lilies of the valley, and outlandish frogs that have dark-green backs and bright-red bellies. On the faces of a number of their rocky cliffs were signs, chalked in red, white, and blue by ROK morale officers, that read, "We are the army of justice," "Our country's thirty million people are waiting for our advance to the north," and so on. Some battalion command posts in the hills, although no more than two air miles distant from their regimental headquarters, were seven hours away—seven hours, that was, for a man whose legs and lungs had become conditioned to alpine exercise. The ROKs, being natives of a predominantly pedestrian and perpendicular land, are better able than most to operate in such terrain. Some of them can march thirty-five miles daily, for days at a time, without being the worse for it. (It was sometimes bitterly observed by units on their flanks that they were not always prone to indulge this talent in a forward direction.) In the fall of 1950, when, for a period, the United States forces were lamentably short of replacements, quite a few South Koreans were integrated by the Eighth Army into American squads, as part of what was known as an augmentation program. When American reinforcements began arriving in more nearly adequate numbers, these Koreans were released to their own Army. By then, many of them had grown so accustomed to traveling about in vehicles that it took them a month to become

116

toughened to the point where they could keep pace with their fellow-citizens.

Along with their remarkable endurance, the ROKs sometimes seemed to have a capacity beyond that of most Americans to withstand pain; at any rate, their medical officers were known to perform amputations in the field without recourse to anesthetics. Most Koreans, whether in or out of the Army, are uncommonly indifferent to suffering—especially other people's—and accept as normal what Americans would consider outright brutality. This is, of course, in the Oriental tradition, and the ROK Army, also following the custom of Oriental armies, was far more partial than any other element of the United Nations forces to maintaining discipline by slaps and punches rather than by, say, letters of reprimand. It was not unusual for generals to dress colonels down by cuffing them, and it was fairly reliably reported—as reliably as anything ever is in a land devoted to myths—that generals had on occasion avoided the tiresome bother of courts-martial by trying, sentencing, and executing a miscreant all at one time. One ROK officer, asked if he didn't think some newly captured and much battered North Korean soldiers at a prisoner-of-war collecting station needed some medical attention, replied, "Oh,

117

they're all right. They all walked three miles to get here. Even that dead one there." Many Korean civilians, too, scored pretty high marks for indifference. They could pass a child whose eye was a bloody pulp without batting one of their own eyes. I can still recall vividly how amazed I was one day by a remark made to me by a well-educated and cultured Korean lady, who had been talking about how she and some other South Koreans had apprehended a North Korean whose known crimes below the Parallel included looting, extortion, and rape. When I asked her what they had done with the culprit, she answered, casually, "Oh, we buried him alive."

A good many Americans in Korea believed that North Korean soldiers, all things considered, fought more skillfully and aggressively than South Korean soldiers, and that they did so because they had been more thoroughly instilled with the will to fight. If the lessons in Communism that North Korean soldiers got were better assimilated than those in democracy given to South Koreans, the chances were it was because any Korean, after living for years in an authoritarian atmosphere, must have found the principles of democracy the more difficult to comprehend, even if expounded to him by the most diligent teachers, which the South Korean soldiers did not always have.

118

One ROK officer, asked how his troops felt about Communism, replied, "I say I hate Communism. Therefore all soldiers I command hate Communism." It is not unlikely that some North Korean general, if asked about his men's attitude toward democracy, would have made a similar response. Actually, the true political inclinations of the less exalted personnel on both sides were hard to gauge. Many South Korean soldiers were unquestionably deficient in political interest. On the other hand, I heard a North Korean prisoner tell an interrogator that all he knew was that he was supposed to be in favor of a man called Kim Il Sung and opposed to one called Syngman Rhee. It's possible that the main difference between the two forces was more a question of tactics than of morale or degree of ideological conviction. The North Koreans had been trained principally in guerrilla fighting; an entire division of them operated for several months deep behind the United Nations lines. The South Koreans had been trained to maintain fixed lines, like American soldiers, and it disconcerted them to have anybody at their rear, with the result that they tried, sometimes disastrously, to get to the rear of the people at their rear.

The North Koreans had even organized lady guerrillas, and the ROKs themselves had a volunteer

Women's Army Corps, and sent their Wacs as far forward as divisional headquarters. The Wacs didn't play an active role in combat, but a couple of them I chatted with at the Capital Division headquarters, where eight of them were on duty, said they were eager to get into the fighting, and, indeed, had enlisted primarily to that end. They had progressed to the point of being issued one hand grenade apiece, but these lone weapons had been taken away from them when the division decided that its masculine standard-bearers required all the ammunition in the vicinity. Accordingly, the Wacs had to confine themselves to administrative and clerical tasks and to serving at the commanding general's mess and tending his flower garden. ROK generals are fond of flowers, and, the season permitting, some flora are usually transplanted to beds around their tents within a few hours after they have set up a new command post.

Not much larger than a South Korean division's quota of Wacs but immeasurably more important to its combat operations was its quota of American officers and men belonging to the Korean Military Advisory Group, or KMAG. During the United States occupation of South Korea, some fifty officers were given the job of assisting in the organization of the Constabulary. They became known as the Provisional

Military Advisory Group, and when the Republic of Korea was established as an independent government, KMAG was set up, with a nucleus of four hundred and forty officers, to give its fledgling Army a helping hand. (The North Koreans were simultaneously benefiting from the counsel of fifteen hundred Russian advisers.) Ultimately there were a thousand of these officers, scattered around Korea wherever there were ROK Army installations or troops. Without them, the ROKs, only about a quarter of whose officers and almost none of whose men possessed even a smattering of English, would have found it impossible to communicate with other United Nations units. (Naturally, nobody hoping to be only temporarily in Korea made much of an effort to learn its language.) KMAG officers were assigned to all ROK tactical units down to battalion level; some of them lived in the inhospitable east-coast hills with the troops for as long as five months at a stretch.

KMAGs, like nearly all other Occidentals, found Korean food unappetizing, and as a result they ran separate messes whenever they could, and they normally occupied separate sleeping quarters. But, even so, they probably came closer than most other Americans to an understanding of the Korean people, and they were generally more sympathetic to the problems of the ROK Army than the men in the other branches of the service were. One KMAG lieutenant colonel, who was an adviser to the ROK chief of staff and accompanied him everywhere, got tired of having to unlace his high boots preparatory to removing them, according to custom, each time he entered a Korean home, and having to lace them up again when he left. He hit upon the notion of using zippers. General Chung, admiring this labor-saving invention, had his own boots altered in the same sensible fashion. After a while, many officers of both nationalities followed suit—an encouraging, if admittedly trivial, indication that East and West could at least occasionally see eye to eye.

9

It was almost inevitable that the Korean War would produce, as it did, the first American jet ace. Soon after the fighting started, our jets made a welcome appearance in the skies, and from then on they were on virtually daily display there, streaking through the air with the sound of them trailing behind the sight of them—a sequence that not infrequently resulted in victims of their lethal attention being hit before they had any idea that there was a machine in the vicinity capable of hitting them. Of three principal kinds of jets with which the Fifth Air Force was equipped, the fastest and most maneuverable was

123

the F-86, or Sabrejet—the type flown by the first ace, Captain James Jabara, and the type that most often clashed with the enemy's celebrated MIGs. (There undoubtedly would have been more American aces if there hadn't been so comparatively few enemy aircraft, other than the elusive MIGs, to tangle with, not to mention if there hadn't been a no-trespassing area north of the Yalu River.) Then there was the F-84, or Thunderjet, and, finally, the F-80, or Shooting Star, the oldest American jet. The F-80, a slender, silvery ship with a fuselage that resembles a cigar wrapped in tinfoil, wasn't used much in air-to-air combat, being, by jet standards, a slow and sluggish vehicle, with a normal cruising speed of scarcely more than four hundred-odd miles an hour, and the ability to turn around only on a nickel. Its "mach number" is a mere .72. The speed of sound—seven hundred and thirty-six miles an hour at sea level at a temperature of fifteen degrees Centigrade —is regarded in the jet world as "mach 1"; the mach number of a jet plane represents that fraction of the speed of sound beyond which it is considered unwise to operate a particular aircraft, since the plane might at that imprudent pace shake itself apart.

Despite the fact that even in a vertical dive an F-80 hardly exceeds five hundred and fifty miles an

124

hour, the F-80 is a sturdy, versatile ship, armed with six fifty-calibre machine guns synchronized with a single trigger. In combat, it is generally fitted out also with rockets, napalm bombs, and perhaps a couple of ordinary thousand-pound bombs, as well as with a cramped pilot who, as he flashes past obscure-looking landmarks beneath him—perched upon a thirty-seven-millimetre projectile that is rigged to propel him abruptly from his seat, should he have to bail out—has to be all at once a skilled driver, scout, engineer, radio operator, and marksman. He also has to be a photographer, but to save him at least some effort his cameras work automatically when his guns do. In Korea, F-80s were mainly employed, as were also quite a few propeller-driven fighters—or "conventional" aircraft, as these old-fashioned types have become known—for close-support missions and for reconnoitering and knocking out enemy ground installations, such as anti-aircraft emplacements, ammunition dumps, and whatnot.

I spent a few days at the home base of one jet outfit, the 49th Fighter-Bomber Group, which in nine months had flown more than twenty thousand combat sorties and, in the course of accounting for seventy-five thousand take-offs and landings at the base, had helped substantially to bring about a rare, and possibly exclusive, accomplishment in the annals of American air warfare. The jets, and the other aircraft using their field, had managed completely to wear out, in that nine-month period, a brand-new strip built by our air engineers. Traffic was so heavy there that one day a sharp-eyed air force colonel, looking things over from the lofty vantage of the strip's operations tower, hadn't even seen one jet crack up as it failed to become airborne during a take-off; so many planes were darting about, and so much dust was being stirred up, that the end of the runway was eclipsed.

During my stay with the 49th, I got especially well acquainted with one of its pilots, a tall, slim captain from Eggertsville, New York, named Fredric F. Champlin, who up to the spring of 1951 had some fourteen hundred hours' flying time to his credit, nearly all of it in fighters. Captain Champlin seemed to me in many ways representative of the typical jet pilot of the Korean War. He is the antithesis of the widespread conception of a fighter pilot as a young, swaggering, devil-may-care hotshot. He is thirty-two years old, married, the father of two children, soft-spoken, cautious, and sedate. He can talk, even about aerial tactics, without waving his arms all over the place and knocking beer mugs off a table. He is quite

126

aware of his being about ten years older than the average fighter pilot was in the Second World War. "Last war I never had anything to do with anybody as old as thirty-two," he told me, "except for one guy who was a group commander, and he looked twenty-six. Of course, even though the guys in my squadron are forever speaking of how elderly some of us are—and early in the war there actually was a pilot flying missions here who was a grandfather—we're really all a bunch of comparatively young men. But being in this line of work makes you feel sort of old." Champlin, who has black hair with a few traces of gray in it, flew a hundred and seventy-five missions during the Second World War, in conventional P-38s. "I was a hotshot then," he said, in a detached, amused way.

The air war in Korea was conducted not without some of the touches of gaiety for which fliers have long been noted. Once when I was near a radio-equipped armored personnel carrier acting as a communications liaison between some ground troops and their tactical air support, a Mosquito swooped low over the vehicle, with which it had been exchanging brief messages, and dropped a well-padded bundle. The crew of the personnel carrier were overwhelmed, on opening it, to find a small bottle of Bourbon, along with a note that said, "Nothing like a shot of Old Forrester in the midst of battle." The squadron to which Champlin has been assigned in Korea still carries on some of the rollicking traditions of the wild old days. It calls itself, for instance, the "Screamin' Demons," and has for its insigne a suitably ferocious-looking demon .that one of its members designed. A pilot from Texas sent his wife there a picture of it, and she obligingly dispatched in return a live horned toad, which, though mute, resembles a demon as much as any other presently living creature, and which was adopted by the squadron as its mascot.

When I met Champlin, early in June, he had never dueled with a MIG, and was inclined to believe he probably never would have that experience. He had seen MIGs in the air a few times, and twice, on spotting flights of six of them (he himself would normally be part of a flight of four F-80s), had turned in on them, hoping for an engagement. But each time this had happened close to the Manchurian border, and each time the enemy had scurried across the Yalu before he could get within range. His first combat mission in a jet took place on January 11, 1950, the day he arrived in Korea from Japan. It was a routine reconnaissance sortie—a search for what are known as targets of opportunity. The only target he

128

saw consisted of two dozen enemy soldiers walking around in the snow. Separated at that moment from his formation, he made a solo strafing pass at the men, and got, he thinks, ten or twelve of them. Then he flew home. Champlin is habitually conservative about making claims. He won't, for instance, take credit for destroying a train unless he has seen its cars completely off the tracks; he won't take credit for a truck unless he has seen it in flames. He did claim a hundred and fifty enemy troops after one mission in April, but, he told me, he had had an exceptionally clear glimpse of his victims; a couple of hundred Communist soldiers had been lounging around in an open courtyard, and he had taken them by surprise. "When we're going after troops in the hills, of course," he said, "we hardly ever know exactly what damage we do."

The difficulty a jet pilot has in accurately appraising the results of his work is largely caused by the pace at which he operates. By the time he has dived down upon a target—descending swiftly from twenty thousand or more feet up to within a hundred feet or less of the ground—he is usually traveling somewhere between four hundred and fifty and five hundred and fifty miles an hour. He has only a couple of seconds to get in his licks. Then, in a hilly country like Korea, he has to pull up sharply, sometimes making an almost vertical climb of five or six thousand feet at the end of his pass. If he slows his plane down for better vision, he loses maneuverability. "Your biggest danger is that you'll concentrate too much on your target," Champlin told me. "Some pilots get what I call 'target fixation.' They'll make their pass and they'll see that their bullets aren't hitting the target right. So they'll start kicking the plane around to try to get lined up with the target, and before they know it they'll be right on top of a mountain, too late to pull up and out."

Another big danger is the effect on a pilot, as he pulls sharply out of a steep dive, of gravitational forces, or "Gs," as the jet men familiarly call them. At such times, the liquids in a man's body flow suddenly from his head toward his feet. His brain and body tissues cannot function properly. Haziness, dizziness, and ebbing consciousness afflict him, in that order. He blacks out. To be sure, he is apt to be completely unconscious for no more than a fraction of a second, but, traveling as rapidly as he does, he can cover quite a bit of territory while his bodily organs are going through this disturbance, and a number of jets have unaccountably slammed into mountainsides while their pilots were trying to pull

130

out of dives. In an attempt to counteract the gravitational pull on them, the Air Force has devised a tight-fitting, girdle-like garment for them, called an anti-G suit, which applies pressure to their abdomens, thighs, bladders, and legs, thereby stemming the rush of blood toward their feet. The use of this garment not only enables them to withstand a couple of Gs more than they might without it, but tends to make the whole experience less exhausting than it would otherwise be. And since a jet pilot, to be efficient, has to be quick-thinking and, like his plane, quick-moving, anything that lessens fatigue is regarded by the Air Force as a boon. Even so, Champlin would often find himself wearier, after a two-hour sortie over Korea, than in the last war he would be after an eight-hour one, in a P-38, over the Philippines or New Guinea.

Of all the missiles in his flying arsenal, Champlin had developed the most respect for napalm, simply because of the destructive power with which this jellied gasoline is endowed. He had no particular compunctions about using it against human beings, whom it is apt to turn into blazing torches. "The first couple of times I went in on a napalm strike," he told me, "I had kind of an empty feeling. I thought afterward, Well, maybe I shouldn't have done it.

Maybe those people I set afire were innocent civilians. But you get conditioned, especially after you've hit what looks like a civilian and the A-frame on his back lights up like a Roman candle—a sure enough sign that he's been carrying ammunition. Normally speaking, I have no qualms about my job. Besides, we don't generally use napalm on people we can see. We use it on hill positions, or buildings. And one thing about napalm is that when you've hit a village and have seen it go up in flames, you know that you've accomplished something. Nothing makes a pilot feel worse than to work over an area and not see that he's accomplished anything. Also, you always know that if you don't do a job, somebody else is going to have to do it. So you might as well do it yourself."

Non-fliers are frequently puzzled as to what it is that drives a pilot to make a solitary assault on an inhospitable target, when he could just as easily bypass it, without anyone's being the wiser, and thereby avoid being shot at and, like as not, being shot down. Champlin has thought about this and has discussed it with other pilots. "I've concluded there may be something odd in the psychological make-up of a fighter pilot," he told me. "Maybe we have a frustration some place. Maybe we're trying to prove something to ourselves about ourselves. Otherwise, I don't know why we go in alone. There are a lot of queer sensations in a job like mine. In the briefing room, being told about a hot target—a rough one, that is— you'll sweat terrifically. As soon as you step into your plane, you become comparatively calm, but not entirely. You're still thinking about all the unpleasant things that could happen to you. But then the moment you see the target, for some reason or other everything is utterly erased from your mind. You go in, and do your job, and if you see a gun on the ground shooting up at you you'll get so mad that you'll go in again, shooting your fifties at it, trying to knock it out, even though the chances may be way against your being able to."

Champlin had flown eighty-five missions in jets by early June, and had fifteen more to go before completing what by then was considered a full tour of duty. In the view of the flight surgeon at his base, a hundred missions was about all that the average pilot could stand, physically and psychologically. Earlier in the Korean War, owing to a shortage of pilots, plenty of men in the Forty-ninth had got well beyond that number, a few of them, in fact, going over the two-hundred-mission mark. But by the time Champlin was nearing his hundredth mission, the

133

flow of replacement pilots from the United States had become sufficiently ample to make it possible for him and others in his position to quit at that point. Owing to the speed of his aircraft and the relatively short distances involved in Korea, he had on several occasions been able to rack up two missions in a single day, the first starting at dawn or even earlier and the second at about two in the afternoon. Most of his missions had been, to his way of thinking, rather uneventful—run-of-the-mill sorties against this or that enemy strongpoint or convoy, from which he hadn't derived much sense of accomplishment. In many instances, he had functioned as little more than an aerial ammunition truck—flying to a designated area, being taken in hand there by a spotter plane, being directed by the spotter, via radio, to bomb or strafe a certain inert-looking hill or cluster of huts, carrying out this assignment faithfully but without seeing any human activity, and then heading back to his base.

But every mission, regardless of how much or how little excitement evolved from it, entailed a lot of work. Before each flight, there was the tedious business of assembling, checking, and donning all his equipment (crash helmet, oxygen mask, and parachute, for instance, in addition to such emergency items, in case he should be forced down or have to bail out, as flares, a mirror, a first-aid kit, a compass, a water bottle, and so on). Then there would be a forty-five-minute briefing, in a room plastered with photographs of pin-up girls craftily placed there by intelligence officers to call the fliers' attention to important advice their eyes might otherwise skip over. He would be given a mission—say to dive-bomb an enemy air strip near Pyongyang. He'd be told what course to follow, and how far away the target was, and what radio aids were available, and what anti-aircraft positions to be on the lookout for. He'd receive appropriate maps and aerial photos, and he'd be brought up to date on what rescue facilities were at the ready should he need them, and he'd be warned again, as he had been many times before, not to cross the Yalu. A ground liaison officer would give him a resumé of the front-line tactical situation, and a weather officer would fill him in on the weather. Then, with the other three pilots in his flight, Champlin would decide how they thought they could best approach the target when they got to it. The chances were that they wouldn't see it, or any other piece of ground, until they were directly upon it, for they would proceed toward it at around twenty thousand feet until, informed by their instruments that they had reached it, they wheeled down. And after each mission, back in the room with the pin-up girls smiling a greeting at them, they'd report to an intelligence officer on what they'd seen and done, or thought they'd done.

After the day's work, there'd be little by way of relaxation that Champlin could do, except go to the movies or have a few drinks at a bar the group maintained at its base. (Japan, a gushing fountain of low-priced potables, was within much easier reach of the Air Force than of the ground troops.) Or he could just lounge around his quarters, a cellular space in a wooden barracks that he had tried to make more comfortable by building a chest of drawers and some shelves out of scrap lumber. (Everybody in Korea had a lot of time on his hands, and many a man with a more or less permanent address and a flair for interior decorating spent a good deal of that time prettying up his home. One foursome of Marine pilots I visited, who occupied a pyramidal tent with wooden half-walls, had fixed the place up with hot and cold running water, built-in bookcases for each bunk, armchairs, and a trap-door in the floor, giving access to an underground shelter that could be used either as a refuge during air raids or as a relatively cool storage spot for beer.)

136

Captain Champlin got into flying largely by accident. The youngest of five children—three boys and two girls—of an upstate New York manufacturer of disinfectants, he attended high school in Buffalo and, after a year's study at the University of Buffalo, went on active military service, early in 1941, as a corporal in a National Guard coast-artillery regiment. While stationed in Georgia, he dropped in on an air base there with a fellow artilleryman who wanted to apply for flying-cadet training. Just for companionship's sake, Champlin filled out an application, too. The friend's was rejected and his was accepted. He attended various schools around the country, ending up in one for fighter pilots—"I seemed to have the right kind of co-ordination for fighters," he told me—and was finally awarded his wings, and the second lieutenant's commission that went along with them, in April, 1943. Two days before he received these, he got married, to his high-school sweetheart. Two months after that, he was shipped to Australia.

Champlin's first combat action in the Second World War occurred on August 6, 1943, when, as part of a squadron of sixteen P-38s, he provided fighter escort for a bunch of air transports carrying supplies up to New Guinea. The P-38s were jumped by twenty-five Japanese Zeros. "I learned later that our squadron got twelve of them," he told me, "but I didn't see any of them go down or who shot them or anything. I was just trying to stay with my leader. I was quite a confused kid." In the next couple of years, as he moved northward through New Guinea and on to the Philippines, he lost that initial sense of confusion, and saw a lot of Zeros go down. He brought down nine himself, thereby becoming an ace. "I also got five on the ground," he said, "but we never counted those, the way they did in Europe." He got his first in September, and one day in November, while participating in a big Allied raid on the port of Rabaul, he got two of them. He ended up with two Distinguished Flying Crosses, eight Air Medals, and the unusual distinction of never being wounded, never having to crash land, never bailing out, and never having a single enemy bullet or fragment of flak hit his plane. His good fortune had stayed with him in Korea, and even though he is a religious man —his wife is a Catholic and he, a Presbyterian for most of his life, took instruction in her faith after their marriage and became converted in 1950—he has no special explanation for his luck. He carries a prayer book and a miraculous medal with him on all flights, but he doesn't think they necessarily deserve full credit, since he didn't have them when he was flying

138

conventional planes. "I can't understand my luck," he told me. "I don't even like to think about it. It's just one of those marvelous breaks."

Champlin returned to the United States in April, 1945, and seven months later, after serving as an instructor of other pilots, reverted to civilian life. He was twenty-seven years old, unskilled in any non-military occupation, and just another of tens of thousands of competent pilots without any occasion to fly. He did try to keep his hand in by once or twice hiring a Cub and taking it up for a spin, but the cost —six dollars an hour—seemed to him excessive, and besides, piloting a Cub was intolerably tame. "To me, it wasn't really flying," he told me. His wife had been working while he was overseas, in an aircraft factory, and between them they had saved some four thousand dollars, so for nearly a year they just took it easy, while he tried to make up his mind what to do —a problem with which quite a few talented and unemployed young aviators were concurrently grappling. Champlin finally resolved to become a dentist; an older brother had established himself in that profession, and it seemed a good field for a man who, in manipulating the myriad tiny switches in a cockpit, had developed excellent co-ordination of his hand muscles. Under the G.I. Bill of Rights, accordingly,

139

he enrolled in a pre-dental course at Canisius College, near his home; he wasn't surprised to find half a dozen other wartime pilots in his class.

But before Champlin had completed his studies, the Korean War broke out, and he was faced with another decision. He had been taking a volunteer air reserve training course, and in the summer of 1950 he received a routine questionnaire asking if he was available for active duty. He knew that he'd go back in, if he did, as a captain, the same rank he'd held at the conclusion of the Second World War. As such, he'd make six hundred and twenty dollars a month, including allowances, a sum that compared invitingly with the three hundred and fifty he was then earning—partly by teaching a laboratory course in botany and zoology at Canisius, partly by working nights as a maintenance man in an arena at Buffalo, and partly from a small pension he had been granted as a result of catching malaria in the Pacific. On the other hand, he had two children by then, and he was hesitant about disrupting their lives. His wife and he, after writing various such pros and cons on a sheet of paper and solemnly analyzing this document for several nights, concluded that he ought to go back in, and late in August he did.

Champlin was assigned to the McGuire Air Base

in New Jersey, adjoining Fort Dix—named in memory of an ace he had flown with during the Second World War—and there had his first introduction to jets when he went up in a T-33, a two-seater variation of the F-80 used for instruction. He was considerably less familiar with jets than are most high-school boys; during the years between wars, he had never bothered to read up on them in technical journals, or any other journals. "I didn't know the first thing about thrusts or tail-pipe temperatures," he told me. "I didn't even know what made the damn things go, and to tell the truth I hadn't been much interested." But he quickly got onto them. "The first big difference I noticed between them and conventional planes," he said, "was that the jets were so much smoother to fly, and that when you were up in one of them, instead of the roar of your engines, you heard only the rush of the air as you swished through it. And then I was amazed at the ease with which you could handle them. A good pilot has to feel that he has absolute control over his airplane, that he can make it do whatever he wants it to. Practically all the controls on a jet are hydraulic; it doesn't take much force to maneuver the plane. I was impressed by the extent to which a man can shove a jet around, and even damage one. Why, I can go up in a jet and

141

wrinkle the devil out of it. With the hydraulic controls, and the strength of my arm, I can, if I'm not careful, warp the plane or tear a wing or the tail off. It's strange to realize you have that much power over a machine."

Champlin didn't expect to be sent overseas right away, but by mid-December he found himself in Japan, flying cover missions over the Dai Ichi Building in Tokyo, where General MacArthur's headquarters were. After a couple of weeks of that protective duty, he requested combat duty in Korea. "I knew it was the one way I could get home," he said. "I wasn't being especially patriotic. I didn't volunteer on behalf of the South Koreans or the United Nations or anything else. I was being purely selfish. I wanted to get home as quickly as possible and I figured getting in combat time was the best way to do it. I've never changed my mind on that score." In Korea, Champlin discovered that flying a jet in battle was relatively little different from flying a conventional plane. The tactical knowledge he had acquired in the war before still stood him in good stead. It was simply a matter of doing everything somewhat faster —like projecting a familiar motion picture at an accelerated rate. There, too, he found many other fighter pilots of his advanced age. Most of them were veterans of the Second World War who, rather than enter the bewildering jungle of civilian life, had elected to stay on in the Air Force. After living with them, and talking with them, for five months, Champlin had just about made up his mind to emulate their example. He was certainly too old, he thought, to entertain any further hopes about dentistry; if he were to stay in the service, he'd be eligible for retirement in another twenty years. His current tour of duty ends in April, 1952, and unless he changes his mind again before then he'll probably make a career of the Air Force. "I know a good deal about jets now," he told me, "but there's still an awful lot I can learn about them. And in the kind of war my generation seems to be perpetually mixed up in, it's not really age that counts, anyway, but experience."

10

W HEN the then Secretary of Defense George Marshall
made an unexpected visit to Korea early in June, 1951
—a trip mysterious in its implications at the time but
one that turned out to antedate only by a few weeks
the start of cease-fire negotiations—he spent a mere
six hours in the country, but even so he made a point
of conferring, however briefly, with every one of the
commanders of the non-American units serving in
combat as part of the Eighth United States Army in
Korea, or, as it was known for short, EUSAK. As was
doubtless his aim, General Marshall by this courteous
gesture drew attention to the fact that the United

144

Nations ground forces had indeed become international in their composition. The Eighth Army's ranks
by then included men from Australia, Belgium, Canada, France, Great Britain, Greece, India, Luxembourg, the Netherlands, New Zealand, the Philippines, Thailand, Turkey, and, of course, the United
States and the Republic of Korea. On hand, too, were
newly arrived ground troops from Colombia and
Ethiopia, as well as air, naval, or hospital units from
Norway, Sweden, Denmark, and the Union of South
Africa. In the United Nations cemetery at Pusan, the
flags of sixteen countries, along with that of the
United Nations, were flying above nearly five thousand graves, as vivid evidence that the cost of collective security had been not only high but widespread.

A British major general remarked after visiting
Korea for the first time that, physically, the place
reminded him of the North-West Frontier country of
India, with perhaps a touch of the vegetation of
Kashmir. Korea may have been thus familiar, at least
on the surface, to some of the hundred officers and
men from India who operated an ambulance unit
there—all of them, by the way, experienced para-
troopers. With that possible exception, the battleground was just as strange to a soldier from, say,
Addis Ababa as it was to any New Yorker, and the

145

non-Americans in the Eighth Army were every bit as afflicted with homesickness as the G.I.s in it, and every bit as eager to go back to wherever they came from. (The hope of rotation was always the biggest single morale booster over there, except, of course, for the Republic of Korea soldiers, who could have no expectation of being rotated to any homes other than the devastated ones past which they were fighting.) The non-Americans blended comfortably into what, although the American influence unquestionably predominated, could truly be described as a polynational and polylingual military operation. One day, while I was riding in an Australian officer's jeep, his driver, an Englishman, obtained traffic directions from a Greek M.P. after establishing that they both had a smattering of Japanese. Korea has become a land of many tongues, and is likely to stay so. Almost every tent or hut occupied by a bunch of United Nations soldiers had a Korean houseboy. The houseboys quickly picked up scraps of their employers' languages, and soon quite a few young Koreans could make themselves understood in French, Thai, Yankee American, Dixie American, or whatever, depending on whose laundry and boots they were looking after. It seems probable that the Republic of

146

Korea, in its future dealings with the rest of the world, will not lack for interpreters.

Apart from the United States and South Korea, which, between them, furnished close to half a million of the soldiers on the scene, no member of the United Nations committed any terribly large amount of manpower to the Eighth Army's resources. Ninety per cent of the graves in the cemetery at Pusan are those of Americans. (In view of the participation just of the South Koreans themselves, however, it seems hardly chivalrous of General Mac-Arthur's chief Intelligence officer to have described the conflict, as he did to an American Legion audience soon after his return to the United States, as an "American" war. This was the same officer who didn't seem to have made his boss aware that the Chinese were in it until too late.) The total strength of the foreign units other than those of the United States was around thirty-five thousand. Of this thirty-five thousand, the British Commonwealth was represented by about twenty thousand and Turkey by five thousand. After that, the numbers fell off sharply, down to the fifty-man task force from Luxembourg that constituted part of the Belgian complement. Most of the smaller contingents were of battalion size, and for operational purposes were assigned to one

American division or another. In several instances, the men in these battalions took to wearing the shoulder insignia of the parent organization, and did so with the enthusiastic approval of the parent organization itself. Before the war, any hard-bitten American trooper of the 1st Cavalry Division would surely have dismissed as absurd the notion that not many months later the gaudy yellow-and-black patch of his aristocratic outfit would be sported on the sleeves of hundreds of citizens of Thailand, but that was to be the case. Many of the adopted soldiers in these outfits also wore patches of their own. The Thais—whose clerks, incidentally, used Remington typewriters with keyboards fitted out with the forty-four letters of the Thai alphabet—were the only ones with a shoulder patch that was created specifically for the Korean War. It consists of their country's conventional insigne with the global blue-and-white design of the United Nations. They were also the only ones with a genuine prince on their roster, His Highness Prince Chalermpolti Kumporn, an amiable captain who slept alone, as befits royalty, in a bright-green tent with built-in, zippered mosquito netting that he had purchased by mail from Sears, Roebuck. It was undoubtedly the only tent of its kind in Korea.

The emblem of the Turkish shoulder patch is the

148

white crescent and white star on a red field of the Turkish flag, and as such is considerably older than the Thais', dating back to 1293, when on the night of a new moon some Turks in battle observed the moon and a single star reflected on the surface of a river that was red with enemy blood. About seventy-five per cent of the Turks, who began fighting in Korea in October, 1950, had lush mustaches, and about one hundred per cent of them acquired the reputation of being exceedingly tough soldiers. When accosted by an M.P. from an allied nation who had caught him in some mischief or other, a Turkish soldier—or so it was commonly reported—would say, "Me Turk," as if that explained everything. Yet the Turks were very docile in the presence of their own officers; none would presume to light a cigarette in the company of a superior, for instance, without first obtaining permission. In battle, the Turks won wide acclaim both for their aggressiveness and for their durability; they took little account of minor injuries, and some of them would treat a bullet wound by simply daubing mercurochrome over the point of entrance. After one spirited engagement, a Turkish officer pointed to a few of his men who had been wounded and were strolling around with assorted fragments of steel still inside them, and said to me

149

proudly, "Some of our men are walking arsenals." When an American officer who had been nicked by shrapnel while serving with these troops in a liaison capacity insisted that the Turkish doctor who attended him make a formal report of his injury, so that he would be eligible for the Purple Heart, the Turks in the vicinity burst out laughing. They thought it was hilarious that anyone could wish to make so much of so little.

The fusion of national interests in Korea, and the attendant intimacy of men from many nations, caused the abatement, if not the complete disappearance, of some long-standing mutual irritations. On the thirty-sixth anniversary of Anzac Day, the D day of the Gallipoli Campaign, in which British and Turks shed not a little of each other's blood, a British brigadier gallantly invited a Turkish brigadier to dinner. Turkey has been traditionally at odds with Greece, too, but when the Greeks were observing their Easter, late in April, one of the warmest messages of fraternal greeting they received from their comrades in arms came from the Turks. The message was transmitted by an American lieutenant from Riverdale, New York, who is fluent in both Greek and Turkish and is representative of the kind of specialist whose

150

services were very much in demand in so special a war.

Although there were, to be sure, plenty of people from each United Nations country, including the United States, who still regarded all the others as ignorant, unintelligible foreigners and had little use for them, the brotherly spirit that flourished in Korea seemed to affect a good many Americans in their intramural relations, with the result that there were signs of co-operation between the various branches of the armed forces that would probably have seemed incredible to even the most ardent Washington advocates of unification. Navy doctors and corpsmen served as medics for Army infantry battalions; in a singular exchange program, several detachments of soldiers spent a few days at sea with the fleet, switching places with sailors, who were thereupon temporarily berthed in foxholes; and when a gob who couldn't swim fell off a ship in the harbor of Pusan, he was saved from drowning by an Air Force lieutenant colonel, who dived in and fished him out.

In the fall of 1950, when the Eighth Army began to assume international proportions, it was thought that many difficulties might arise in catering to the peculiar needs of its varied components, especially with regard to dietary habits and preferences. These

151

difficulties did not materialize. Aside from the British, who had their own uniforms, weapons, transportation, and supply lines, nearly all the non-American units were logistically dependent wholly or in major part on the United States, which sold them whatever they needed to keep their troops going and found them, in general, perfectly satisfied with American food. The Turks, who are, of course, Mohammedans and sometimes went into an attack shouting "Allah!" (the Greeks shouted "Aera!" or "Give me air!"), have religious scruples against pork and personal scruples in favor of olive oil and bread. (They are also supposed to have religious scruples against alcoholic spirits, but, like most soldiers, they are inclined to drink anything they can get their hands on anyway.) Accordingly, in addition to fresh food when it was available, the Turks were supplied with a special, pork-free C ration, gallons of olive oil to cook everything in, and two pounds of bread per man daily. The French baked the bread for their troops—French bread, naturally. The Filipinos, although partial to rice, didn't take to the local variety, and had their own shipped up from Manila. The Thais, who are extravagantly fond of hot sauces, were issued—and consumed—two and a half ounces of tabasco per man per week. (The standard table-size bottle of tabasco, which lasts most American families for months, contains two ounces.) One of the most unusual requests for special rations, to the Eighth Army's way of thinking, was put in during the spring by the Greeks, who, in anticipation of their Easter, asked for some live sheep, so they could celebrate the occasion with the customary sacrifice. The United Nations Command obligingly had a flock of fifteen tender lambs sent by airlift to Korea from Japan. It is also customary for the Greeks to enliven Easter by banging together the ends of hard-boiled eggs that have been dyed red, the theory being that the person whose egg doesn't break is destined to enjoy a year's good luck. General Van Fleet, whose previous experience in the conduct of ostensibly civil wars had been gained in Greece, turned up during the Greeks' Easter ceremonies—which were held, however inappropriately, in the courtyard of the Seoul municipal jail, where the Hellenic forces' command post happened to be just then—and, after duly clicking an egg proffered by the Greeks' senior officer, proceeded to pull off what was certainly one of the most gracious diplomatic coups of the war. "Now let's try *my* eggs," said Van Fleet, and, while the assembled Greeks looked on with wondering admiration, one of his aides stepped forward with a soda-cracker box full of red-dyed eggs, which the Army commander had forehandedly brought along.

In proportion to their strength, the non-American and non-Korean soldiers in the Eighth Army suffered a stiff number of casualties; they also—in the case of the British, the Dutch, and the French—won unit citations for extraordinary achievements in battle, and, all things considered, made a substantial contribution to the Eighth Army's accomplishments. Early in June, when one of the Army's corps finally succeeded in seizing two prime objectives—the cities of Chorwon and Kumhwa—the vanguard of the occupying troops was composed of Americans, Greeks, Turks, Filipinos, and Thais. Three weeks before that, the French and the Dutch had played a notably helpful part in beating back the big attack the Chinese threw at the American 2nd Infantry Division. A few weeks before that, an observer proceeding along the Eighth Army's front from west to east in search of a North American unit would have had to travel quite a few miles before encountering one, and en route would have passed South Koreans, Filipinos, Puerto Ricans, Britons, and Turks, all fighting flank to flank and giving an impressively united account of themselves. In view of such collaborative performances as those, the idea won favor in some circles—includ-

154

ing the highest diplomatic circles, if not, at least publicly, the highest military ones—that there could have been no more fitting way of recognizing the unique character of General Van Fleet's command than by changing its name from EUSAK to FUNA, an abbreviation that, no matter how the Russians might have tried to explain it, would always be remembered as standing for First United Nations Army.

IN KOREA, as in other sections of the world where American servicemen have strutted their stuff, there was often to be found a certain lack of sympathetic understanding between the visitors and the home folks. The Korean people are not yet universally conditioned to the presence in their midst of outsiders, and particularly ones from the Western world. Until a dozen years or so before the end of the nineteenth century, when some American missionaries established their first beachhead in the country, hardly any United States citizens had ever been there. (Probably close to half a million Americans have

156

attained this no longer exclusive distinction in recent months.) The Koreans are understandably leery of foreigners, inasmuch as most of the outlanders to arrive within the last several centuries have stayed on as occupiers. The Japanese assumed that role for nearly the entire first half of the twentieth century, and the Koreans, who in pride and self-respect seem to tower over their neighbors from Nippon, are far less inclined nowadays to take a forgiving view of their one-time humiliaters than are, say, most of the Americans presently in Japan. Consequently, it has lately been the discreet practice of most Japanese firms having business dealings in Korea to send to that country, as their emissaries, not Japanese, who would be coolly received, but Americans.

Many a traveling American, in or out of uniform, looks upon people who do not wear Western-style clothes and do not favor steak and French-fried potatoes over all other foods as not merely peculiar but absolutely benighted. By this arbitrary sort of criterion, most Koreans strike most Americans as being very odd indeed. The majority of Koreans still live just about the way they did many, many years ago and are partial to their country's traditional diet: rice, a throat-searing pickled salad called *kim chi,* bean curd, and, on special occasions, such fancy

157

dishes as half-raw chickens brought to the table with their heads on. *Kim chi* and bean-curd soup, not to mention wholly raw fish, are just as likely to appear on a table at breakfast-time as at any other hour. Most of the Americans in Korea rarely got to sample the native fare, at any hour. There were not many restaurants even in such large communities as Pusan and Taegu that looked terribly inviting, and not many private homes whose occupants were in a position or in a mood to do any entertaining.

There are exceedingly few residents of either South or North Korea whose lives have not been intimately touched by the war. I paid a call one afternoon on one South Korean farmer who had been affected less than most. His name is Bak Pyung Choon and he lives in the village of Tangnidong, a placid settlement of a hundred and sixty families located in the region between Taegu and Pusan, one of the few parts of Korea that has not been the scene of any ground fighting. Bak is a tall, thin man, fairly dark complected, with long, tapering, gray hands, and a gray mustache and beard the tip of which is delicately braided. He was sixty-one years old at the time of my visit. Sixty-one is regarded by the Koreans as an especially estimable year, and accordingly he was wearing a handsome silk costume—all white ex-

158

cept for a gray brocade waistcoat—that the eldest of his four sons had given him as a birthday present on the occasion of his reaching that revered anniversary. Bak had lived in the village for fifty years; he was born in another village seven miles away. The longest trip he had ever made away from his home district had been a journey to Seoul, a couple of hundred miles away, thirty years before, when he had gone to the capital to take in a fair. He had never seen an American before, to the best of his knowledge. Aside from the passage of thirty refugees through his house, at one time or another since the fighting began, and aside from his having been harshly affected by inflation and high taxes, the war had scarcely changed his life. His home, which he had built himself fourteen years earlier, consisted of three huts—made of wooden beams plastered with clay and roofed with thatch—built around a court-yard that had a well in the center of it. In the yard outside his front door were five persimmon trees and a *sansuyu* tree, the leaves of which he and his fellow villagers use for medicine. An ox was tethered outside, and near it were a black goat and a couple of a species of dog peculiar to Korea—a cross, seemingly, between a German shepherd and a fox terrier. The thin interior partitions of Bak's home were being

159

repapered, which he told an interpreter I had brought along was an annual occurrence, sort of like spring cleaning. Wearing the black horsehair skull cap that Korean elders don indoors and sitting cross-legged on a gaily-colored pillow, Bak offered me an unopened pack of Old Golds. Another Korean had given them to him, he said, but he didn't smoke cigarettes, preferring to stick to a two-foot long bamboo pipe with a tiny silver bowl. His home was spotlessly clean and simply furnished—some mats to sleep on, pillows to sit on, a kerosene lamp, a couple of low tables inlaid with mother-of-pearl, a handsome chest of inlaid wood, and, on a wall behind him, two framed pictures a son had given him. One was a sample of Oriental leg art; the other showed a man and a woman with heads bowed, standing in a rice paddy, as if praying for their land. It seemed appropriate, for if anything is to sustain the South Koreans during the next few years, their fertile soil will undoubtedly have to be it.

Bak had never been to school, but he had taught himself to read and write both Korean and Chinese. He had a few books around, one on Chinese history, another on Korean politics, and a third on old-time etiquette—a volume expounding the proper method of conducting funerals, weddings, and other impor-

160

tant ceremonies. Bak received no news of current events either from newspaper or radio reports, but he had kept abreast of recent history partly by talking in the village square and partly by listening to one of his sons, a member of the South Korean police, who got around and who visited him from time to time. The father had been following the war closely and with interest, though the latest information he had on it when I saw him was a month old. He had a fairly high opinion of Syngman Rhee and a fairly low one of Communism. He said he didn't know much about Communism, but that it was his understanding that under it, in theory, a man was supposed to get paid according to how much he worked, and that, in practice, a man didn't necessarily get paid for his work. Bak didn't like that duplicity. Furthermore, he believed that the Communists made old men like himself work, and forbade sons to work for their fathers. He didn't like that impertinence, either. He hoped that the war would end soon, but had no opinion how or when it would. He said that Russia had started it over a disagreement with the United States, that each nation wanted to have its own way, and that he personally was a pawn involved in the struggle and, no matter how he might feel about it, couldn't

161

possibly expect to have any influence on its out-
come. He had never heard of the United Nations.

Bak Pyung Choon was an exceptionally lucky
Korean. The good fortune his village enjoyed was
typified by the fact that one of its inhabitants was,
during my visit, building himself a new house, not
because he had no place to live but simply because
he wanted a bigger house than his old one. Many
Korean farmers had no place to live and no immediate hope of finding any. Yet they hung around
the valleys and fields familiar to them, sometimes
even if a spirited fire fight was going on in the
neighborhood. The blithe disregard many of them
showed toward flying missiles may have resulted
from a feeling on their part that, already having
suffered as much as they had, it didn't much matter
whether they were hit or not. Or it may have resulted
simply from their stolidity, a trait that Koreans displayed—often startlingly and sometimes infuriatingly
—far behind the battle lines, too. You'd think that a
resident of a municipality like Taegu, after months
of ceaseless exposure to the rumble of military traffic
along his streets, would at least glance briefly around
him before undertaking to cross one. But no; Koreans
step out into the path of a heavy truck just as fool-
ishly and foolhardily as if they were native New

Yorkers. One clear and cloudless day, coming into an airstrip outside Taegu in a Navy torpedo bomber in which I had hitched a ride cross country, I was puzzled when, just as our wheels were about to touch down, the pilot gunned his engine and pulled up in the air. Later I asked him what had happened. "Oh, nothing special," he said. "Just some Koreans ambling out across the runway. They do it all the time."

By no means all Koreans are so apparently indifferent, however, to what is going on around them, or swooping down on top of them. Most of them, especially the younger ones, are quick to pick up things by observation and imitation. Throughout Korea, wherever an American unit had encamped for any length of time, could be found Korean children going through the motions, quite realistically, of playing baseball or of boxing. Some Koreans also became shrewdly aware that many of the United Nations soldiers were partial to stimulants, and accordingly there appeared everywhere various home-made brews —some dispensed in old Coca-Cola bottles and others in unidentifiable, but patently not brand-new, containers—which were hopefully offered for sale to passing soldiers. A chemical analysis made in Pusan of one such nectar found it to consist about half and

163

half of human urine and methyl alcohol. Not all the native distillations were so unappetizing, or so dangerous. At Kyongsang, some twenty miles south of Taegu, I once visited the home of a wealthy family that owned a flock of apple orchards and also the Paik Sun Distillery Company, where they bottled a beverage called Oriental Apple Brandy. I was courteously asked to sample it, and it was most agreeable —as nice a little unpretentious apple brandy as you could expect to find anywhere. In the absence, however, of any reasonable minimum standard of quality for bottled goods, the United Nations authorities felt impelled every now and then to search all vehicles for and confiscate all indigenous spirits—not excepting even, I suspect, my Oriental Apple Brandy. This precaution was eminently sensible, for there were several instances of thirsty soldiers dying in suspiciously short order after sampling one unlabeled brand or another.

If the United Nations forces felt little gratitude toward their involuntary hosts for such lethal assaults upon their stomachs, they felt even less for the decidedly inhospitable practice by some Koreans of, while clothed like civilians, carrying weapons and ammunition of considerably deadlier potentiality. I never saw an outwardly innocuous passerby unfrocked

164

and exposed as a walking arsenal, but I heard enough of such incidents from reliable sources to be convinced that they had occurred, especially toward the start of the hostilities. Whenever any deception of this sort was revealed, news of it spread rapidly, and left behind it a seething wake of bitterness and resentment. This distrust, blended in equal parts with the traditional contempt of many Americans for all non-Americans, produced somewhat strained relations between the two principal allies in the war. The use by most Americans of the word "gook" as descriptive of all Koreans probably didn't help much to smooth things over, although I doubt whether the Koreans themselves were overly distressed by that characterization. They called Americans "gooks," too—using the word simply to connote "foreigner"— and it was not unusual for KMAG officers attached to ROK units to identify themselves at night, if hailed by a sentry and unacquainted with the evening's password, by cheerfully calling out, "Me gook."

Our armed forces did try from time to time to foster a spirit of fraternalism between Americans and Koreans. Information-and-education experts were forever circulating pictorial appeals for brotherly love. One poster, showing a jeep driver impatiently glaring at a Korean pedestrian, bent over with a

165

loaded A-frame on his back, who was blocking his way, was captioned, "Keep your shirt on. After all, it's his road." Another, showing an elderly Korean man staring solemnly at a G.I., was captioned, "He may forget the face. He'll always remember the uniform." What effect, if any, such exhortations had is hard to guess; Korea became so plastered with signs of one kind or another that the majority of G.I.s probably gave those particular two, if they noticed them at all, no more than a glance. Cumulative sign messages of the Burma-Shave school were among the most popular of those on exhibit along the roads. One four-part warning that cropped up every few miles, it seemed, went, "Slow down, Joe—Curve ahead—No rotation—If you're dead." Even the Koreans themselves adopted this device, though forgoing the rhymes. Tacked to telegraph poles and trees on the main avenue leading into Seoul from the south were such hand-lettered sentiments, arranged so as to be read by someone moving north, as "We— All—Thank—You," "Koreans—Thank—U.N.," and "Long—Live—Freedom." Korean sign-painters, notably those who could cope with English letters, were among the few occupational groups in the country to keep busy during a period of economic chaos, for the towns where Americans installed themselves rapidly became festooned with notices put up by the local population for foreign view. About half of these were displayed outside establishments that, whatever their pre-war function, had shifted to the laundry business, and some of these signs reflected the difficulty that Oriental businessmen so often have when seeking to advertise their services in Occidental lingo. "Speed and Kind," one laundry in Taegu proclaimed outside its door; another shop, a few blocks away, boasted so all could see that its slogan was "Minimum Quality —Maximum Price."

Since most Koreans had no better grasp of English than had the earnest but misguided proprietor of that laundry, and since practically no Americans had any grasp of Korean at all, there was no chance of members of the two groups sitting down together and chatting about their differences. There has undoubtedly been less social intercourse—or, for that matter, any other kind of intercourse—between Americans and Koreans than between Americans and the natives of any other region to which we have lately migrated in armed force. Most Americans were singularly uninterested in trying to learn anything about Korea's venerable history, or to understand any of its ancient customs. Once, traveling by jeep from Taejon to Taegu, I saw a funeral procession moving along a

167

paddy dike just off the road, and asked my driver to stop. It was a colorful sight. The deceased was being transported to his grave in an elaborate and many-hued casket, surmounted by a gaudy canopy, that was carried by fifteen pall-bearers, all marching in perfect step in keeping with a stately rhythm set by a bell-ringer who trudged along some fifteen feet ahead of the rest of the mourners. As they marched by, they chanted what sounded like "Ho—ho—ho—oooo," one syllable per step. My jeep driver remarked that it was the silliest damn funeral procession he had ever seen. I ventured the suggestion that to a Korean a convoy of polished Cadillac or Packard limousines might seem just as silly a performance, but the driver was unimpressed, and retorted that it was obvious that Korea would never amount to anything as long as its citizens persisted in such follies.

A few miles farther along the road, one of our tires went flat. Having no tools with us, we bumped along until we came upon a roadside maintenance hut manned by several Koreans in ROK Army uniforms. We stopped, and my driver curtly ordered the ROKs to attend to the tire. While they were getting set, he walked into their hut and looked around. On coming out, he asked one of the Koreans, who understood a little English, for a pressure gauge, so he could

168

check the air in the other tires. The Korean said he didn't have a gauge. My driver got furious. He said he had seen one inside the hut, and that the Korean was a liar and a scoundrel for denying its presence there. The Korean replied calmly that the gauge in question was a broken one. The driver returned to the hut, got the gauge, brought it back out, and attached it to one of the tire valves, cursing all the while at the Korean's deceitfulness. The Korean watched him, smiling. When the fact that the gauge was worthless dawned on the American, the Korean began laughing; it was pretty ludicrous to see the man struggling obstinately with a gadget that he had already been assured wouldn't work. The driver, all the more infuriated at having become an object of mirth, was for slugging the Korean who had presumed to laugh at him, and he would have, too, if the other ROKs hadn't just then finished changing his tire. He climbed back behind the wheel and drove off, without uttering a word of thanks for the help he'd been given. I mention this minor incident in such detail only because, unfortunately, it was a far from atypical example of the way some of our men abroad who could have been ambassadors of good will managed instead to be exactly the opposite.

One trait of the Korean people that incensed many

169

Americans was their carefree attitude toward other people's property. Theft in a war zone is always considered almost as much a sport as a crime, and the practice of it in Korea was by no means confined to any single group—one ROK Army unit, after bivouacking for a couple of days close to an American regiment, reported five of its jeeps and two two-and-a-half-ton trucks missing—but the Koreans, who had very little property of their own aside from what they got from their U.N. associates, went in for it with somewhat greater gusto than any others on the scene. American officers on duty with ROK combat units had the letters "KMAG" stamped through the metal on one side of their jeeps, on the theory that this ineradicable evidence of ownership might inhibit their disappearance. (In a photograph I saw after returning home of some of the Communist delegates to the Kaesong meetings seated in an American jeep—the caption noted that it was uncertain how the jeep had fallen into enemy hands—I could see the letters "KMAG" on the vehicle, so I was fairly certain at least out of whose hands it had fallen in the first place.) A similar tactic was employed on occasion by Koreans themselves. Three houseboys attached to one American unit, the grateful recipients both of some white T-shirts and some atabrine tablets,

170

had used the latter not to ward off malaria but to dye the former a bright yellow. Their explanation was that they wanted to make the garments conspicuous enough to dissuade any other Koreans from filching them.

Soon after the United Nations recaptured Seoul in March, the market places there were full of native venders offering, at fantastically low prices, elegant wares that had undoubtedly graced private homes in the city. It seemed scarcely possible that all the people putting them up for sale had occupied the houses from which they had been removed. A great many Americans deplored the questionable morality of such transactions; some of those who deplored the loudest were quickest to take advantage of the bargain prices. And some Americans were also the least willing to recognize the fact that, with hardly any jobs available in Seoul, a Korean who needed money to buy food for his family was often faced with the simple choice of stealing or starving. As one ROK Army officer put it to me, while ruefully discussing some of the difficulties he had encountered in trying to make his allies from abroad comprehend the plight of his countrymen, "A rich man never knows a poor man's hunger."

12

Practically all roads in Korea lead, however bumpily, to Pusan, a seaport that for a time seemed on the point of becoming an Oriental Dunkirk. Pusan, at the southeast edge of the peninsula, and Taegu, slightly over a hundred miles to its north, are the only large cities of Korea physically undamaged by the war. Taegu, which had a prewar population of around two hundred thousand, was one year later housing, in a manner of speaking, about three times that number. Pusan, which had a prewar population of around half a million, contained about twice that. It was almost impossible to arrive at more precise figures; estimates

172

of the number of refugees who came to Pusan from the north, for instance, ranged, even in supposedly informed circles, all the way from two hundred thousand to more than a million. In the course of the war, nearly everybody involved in Korea's anguished current history moved through or into Pusan. The government of the Republic of Korea, with its attendant embassies and legations, has been in residence there since its evacuation from Seoul at the start of 1951. A Northwest Airlines agent who had to flee Seoul himself at that time, and in doing so lost track of a limousine he had used to ferry passengers to and from the airport, was not terribly surprised nearly a year afterward to discover that the missing vehicle had also migrated to Pusan; stripped of its wheels and its engine, it was serving as a home for two refugee families. There are streetcars running in Pusan that used to ply the tracks of Atlanta, Georgia; they were shipped to the port by courtesy of E.C.A. There are also rare private automobiles, some of them so aged and decrepit that their wheels seem to wobble sidewise as much as they roll forward. There are busy rail yards and a fine, spacious harbor—a bay flanked by handsome hills. The city's southerly location and its ample piers—which, like almost all other important facilities in prewar Korea, were constructed by

173

the Japanese—made it the chief funnel for the United Nations forces' seaborne logistic support. Fresh troops being shipped to the combat areas, and tired ones being rotated out, generally passed through there. Since, despite the attractiveness of its setting, it is a dingy, dusty, and unpleasantly fragrant community, the men were usually delighted to get beyond it, whichever way they were heading.

Clinging to the sides of the hills that rise in the center of the city are hundreds of shacks, built out of cardboard and paper by refugees unable to find more substantial shelter. Many of these people hailed from Seoul, and they were much relieved to hear in the late spring of 1951 that their government and the Eighth Army were firmly committed to a policy of allowing no refugees to settle in Seoul. This restriction meant, for one thing, that the permanent residents of Seoul temporarily located elsewhere could hope to find their homes, on their eventual return, if not in awfully good shape, at least not occupied by squatters, who might invoke the old argument about possession's being nine points of the law.

Throughout Korea, by the time the war had been going on almost twelve months, there were somewhere between three million and six million people who were adrift from their homes. In many instances,

174

they were absolutely destitute, although they were on the whole much better off in the warm weather than they had been the previous winter, when sub-zero temperatures had been added to their other hardships. The allotment of such succor as they had—principally, a pound of rice daily apiece—was handled in large measure by their own federal, provincial, and village officials, under the supervisory eye of the United Nations Civil Assistance Command in Korea. UNCACK, operating under Army control, was composed about half and half of military and civilian personnel, many of the latter recruited from the World Health Organization, the International Refugee Organization, and the various global branches of the Red Cross. A typical UNCACK field team would consist of an American Army officer, a Scottish doctor, a Swedish welfare man, and a Peruvian sanitary engineer. Partly because of the philanthropic travels of such units as these, partly because of the natural hardiness of the Korean people, and partly because of the admirable resistance displayed by many local officials to the human temptation to skim off a little of whatever material aid came their way, there had been no serious malnutrition in the country since the fighting began, and, what was perhaps even more remarkable, none of the diseases

175

endemic to this part of the world had yet become pandemic. The lengths to which the government and UNCACK have gone to head off widespread illness were demonstrated in Pusan, where within three months seven hundred thousand Koreans were vaccinated against smallpox. "That's nowhere near as impressive statistically as what you did in New York a few years back," one UNCACK doctor, a Mexican, told me in Pusan one day. "But in New York practically everybody understood what vaccination was all about, and went willingly to have it done. Here, where we have to cope with ignorance, we were obliged to seek out the population block by block and house by house. The mountain wouldn't come to us. We had to go to the mountain."

All over the southern Korean mainland, and on several of the islands to the south of it, refugee camps were set up to provide shelter for those homeless folk who had failed to find it with friends or with hospitable strangers. I looked in on one such installation in Pusan, on the site of what used to be the National Veterinary Quarantine Station, an asylum for indisposed cattle. Five thousand refugees were quartered there at the time of my visit, but their residential status was uncertain, for their particular governmental patron, the Minister of Social Affairs, was cur-

176

rently at odds with the Minister of Agriculture over the question of whether the place should continue to be made available to them or should revert to suspect cows. The accommodations I saw were of a sort that a fastidious dairy farmer in Wisconsin would certainly reject as sub-par. In one fifty-foot-long, sunless mud hut with a dirt floor and a thatched roof, surrounded by ditches buzzing with flies, ninety-seven people were living. Families of six were jammed into compartments measuring eight feet by six and separated from adjacent ones only by rice-sack curtains. There was no screening for the community kitchens—a couple of iron pots sitting over open fires—or for the community latrines, which were, to put it mildly, primitive. In the midst of such disadvantages, the inhabitants of the camp were doing their best to keep their huts tidy and to carry on some sort of social life. In one cattle shed, a school was in session, with a student body of four hundred and a faculty of four. The teachers, themselves refugees, had hardly any textbooks, but they did have a few blackboards, and the lessons they had chalked on these were being diligently copied by their pupils into notebooks made from the cardboard sides of ration cartons. The camp contained a hospital, too, consisting of a ward set up in the headquarters

177

building of the quarantine station, and fifteen tents scattered around outside. Within each tent were some two dozen patients, arrayed on the ground on litters. The hospital's staff—six Korean doctors, with extremely scanty equipment—had to care for as many as two hundred and forty-five incoming patients a day, many of them civilians who had been caught in an artillery barrage or a bath of napalm.

In unavoidably striking contrast to that hospital was one I visited the following day, in another camp for displaced persons—the persons in this case being North Korean and Chinese prisoners of war. Behind the ring of barbed wire that enclosed this camp was a huge hospital with considerable equipment and facilities, including a dental clinic and an eye, ear, nose, and throat clinic, the latter complete with illuminated vision charts bearing Korean characters, got up by the American Army administrators of the place. Twenty-three American doctors were on duty when I dropped in, and I found that most of them, regardless of their feelings about their charges' previous activities, were pleased with at least one aspect of their assignment—it was giving them the chance, enjoyed by few physicians in the United States, to observe at first hand the symptoms of such interesting ailments as hemorrhagic smallpox and leprosy. About the only thing the prison hospital had in common with the refugee hospital, aside from the universality of pain, was that head cases requiring especially delicate surgery were referred from both places—as were similar cases among United Nations soldiers— to a specialist from Copenhagen who was based aboard a Danish hospital ship and who operated with impartial skill on damaged brains that in their sounder state had entertained all kinds of dissimilar notions about the causes and probable effects of the war.

A singular feature of the prisoner-of-war camp— where the living conditions provided for the healthy inmates by the United Nations Command were like- wise incomparably better than those the South Ko- rean government could afford to furnish its refugees —was the presence in it of six hundred women pris- oners, many of them accompanied by their children, and some of them nursing infants born in the camp after unusually confined confinements. A number of these women, who ranged in age from schoolgirls to grandmothers, explained their situation by claiming to be Army nurses. Others claimed to be soldiers' wives who couldn't refrain from following their hus- bands into combat, or to be plain civilians, either North or South Korean in origin, who just happened to be taking a trip through the battle lines. The word "nurse" is apparently used rather elastically in the Orient; some of these captive nurses, while not markedly adept at adjusting bandages, admitted to a good deal of experience in toting ammunition. It was an odd experience, after walking through the main part of the prison camp and seeing thousands of male Chinese and North Koreans—who were kept segregated, inasmuch as they seemed to have little affection for each other—to come suddenly upon the women's compound, where children played animatedly in the dirt while their mothers sewed or crocheted to pass the time away. Some of the women were fairly tough characters who, during intracamp spats, showed themselves less apt to scratch or pull hair than to go after one another with rocks. But others, more in the tradition of their sex, had made ladylike efforts to pretty up their tents; over one prisoner's cot I noticed two colored pictures tacked up—a drawing of a Madonna and Child with Asian features, and an advertisement, clipped from an American magazine, in which a handsome young couple were clinging together in a fervent embrace.

Many of the male prisoners devoted hours to creating *objets d'art* out of beer cans, surely not the most pliable of materials. They turned out ornamental wastebaskets, ash trays, and cigarette cases, as well

180

as flowerpots with tin flowers in them. Some of the
tin flowers even had tin butterflies perched on their
stiff petals. The United States Brewers Foundation
may not be aware of it, but quite a few Koreans, no
matter which side of the Thirty-eighth Parallel or the
barbed wire they hail from, are addicted to fashion-
ing things out of beer cans. In several Korean cities,
I saw shops in which children's sand pails made from
beer cans were displayed. While calling at a Catholic
orphanage in Taegu, I was taken to the dining hall,
where two long tables had been set for the evening
meal. There were about a hundred places at the
tables, and at each was a plate and, as a cup, a Bal-
lantine's beer can with its top sliced off. I don't know
why this orphanage went in for that brand exclusively; there may have been other institutions nearby
partial to Schlitz or Pabst.

Among the people blended into the melting pot
of Pusan were a great many who were preoccupied
with the problem of what was going to happen to
Korea when, if, and however hostilities ceased. For
example, the Ministry of Social Affairs, in view of the
fact that from two hundred and fifty thousand to
four hundred and twenty thousand dwellings had
already been demolished in the Republic (it was just
as difficult to get an exact count of ruined homes as

181

of ruined human beings), had had blueprints drawn up for three kinds of house—urban, village, and farm —whose construction the government proposed to subsidize as soon as possible. (It was expected that a Korean farmer, given window sills, door frames, tools, and plans, would be able to build an adequate stone-and-earth lodging for three hundred thousand *won*, or fifty dollars.) No one was more deeply concerned about the resurrection of this land than the representatives of the United Nations in Pusan, for the U.N. was not only responsible for the birth of the nation but seems likely to have it as a rather helpless ward for some time. Korea has plenty of natural resources (coal and gold among them), good ports, and, by Oriental standards, a good road network. The country's economy is primarily agrarian, sixty per cent of its annual income in normal times being derived from its rice crop; even in 1950, South Korea exported a hundred thousand tons of rice to Japan. But the country is woefully short of citizens with industrial experience. The Japanese, during their occupation, allowed few Koreans to be initiated into the mysteries of running a business enterprise. Under the present constitution, practically all the major industries that the Japanese once supervised have been nationalized, but there aren't enough competent Koreans to manage them, and not many of them were self-sustaining even before the fighting began. Thanks to the war, seventy per cent of South Korea's industrial potential has been shattered. The war, furthermore, has contributed to a serious inflation. By the summer of 1951, prices were more than eight times what they were three years before. The government was badly in debt and it seemed inevitable that it would go in deeper, partly because of a tax system that was regarded by visiting economists as inadequate and poorly administered. South Korea has already received substantial non-military aid from the outside world, including more than a hundred million dollars' worth of goods and services from the United States. And there have been gifts from other nations, too—five thousand metric tons of sugar from Denmark, about the same amount of salt from England, two thousand cases of laundry soap from Greece and eight thousand cases of it from New Zealand, a hundred tons of raw rubber from Liberia, and so on. But the country will need a great deal more help in the years to come.

Two United Nations agencies besides UNCACK were in Pusan to give what help they could. One was the United Nations Commission for the Unification and Rehabilitation of Korea, or UNCURK, which functioned mainly in the political sphere; the other was the United Nations Korean Reconstruction Agency, or UNKRA, whose province was economics. UNCURK, a seven-nation commission composed of representatives from Australia, Chile, the Netherlands, Pakistan, the Philippines, Thailand, and Turkey, had been in Korea since November, 1950, when its members arrived at Seoul with the heady impression that the war was about finished and that their principal task—achieving unification—could be tackled almost immediately. Two days after their arrival, they were compelled to lower their sights as a result of General MacArthur's revelation that the Chinese had entered the war. Consequently, UNCURK's efforts toward unification had to be mostly reflective. There was the question to ponder, for example, of whether Communists should be permitted to vote in any elections that might be held jointly in North and South Korea, and, if so, whether the Communist Party, understandably outlawed south of the Thirty-eighth Parallel, should be permitted to put up candidates. On a more practical and less remote level, UNCURK, like UNCACK, was busying itself with such matters as the procurement of food and fertilizer and the rehabilitation of certain branches of the ROK government. The United Nations had no

184

direct authority over the government—after all, South Korea's sovereignty was proclaimed with the special blessing of the United Nations—but it tactfully proffered some ameliorative suggestions, which were adopted. In December, 1950, for instance, after ROK soldiers and police in Seoul had executed some other Koreans "in a little too great quantity and a little too visibly," as one UNCURK man discreetly put it to me, the commission persuaded President Rhee's government to modify its disciplinary practices, with the healthy result that there were few visible executions thereafter. UNCURK also succeeded in establishing and maintaining more cordial relations with the American military forces here than prevailed under General MacArthur, who was occasionally inclined to take a paternal rather than a filial view of the organization under whose banner his troops were deployed. The rapport between the United Nations and General Ridgway, who for a couple of years served at the head of the American Army staff mission at Lake Success, was what a usually reserved UNCURK man described to me as "super-excellent."

The United Nations Korean Reconstruction Agency was promised a budget of two hundred and fifty million dollars by the General Assembly (part cash and part gifts in kind) for its first year of operations, but not all the forty-two nations that offered to contribute to this fund came across immediately. According to Sir Arthur Rucker, the Deputy Agent-General of UNKRA and its highest official in Korea during my stay there, the job of repairing Korea, even if the entire amount proved to be forthcoming, would depend mainly on the Koreans. "All we can do," he told me one day, "is to try, intelligently and generously, to help them help themselves. If we accomplish that, it will be a partial fulfillment of the United Nations charter." To the end of obtaining the right kind of help, the South Korean government asked UNKRA to enlist and import expert advisers in fifty-three specialized fields, among them harbor dredging, bridge building, water supply, tungsten refining, fish canning, pharmaceutics, telephone and telegraph communications, finance, and prison supervision. UNKRA planned to fill this panel as rapidly as it could find people who were suitable and available. One specialist whose presence the Koreans requested but who it was feared might not be too easy to dig up was an expert in a field described by the petitioning government as "decommunization." Whoever he might be, a man with proved ability in that line would undoubtedly be considered handy by quite a number of uncertain governments today.

13

In the days preceding June 25, 1951, the first anniversary of the outbreak of the fighting, there was in Korea, as there is on the eve of any birthday anywhere, a good deal of speculation about what surprises might turn up on the big day. Would there be, for instance, an augmentation of the enemy's nightly harassing of our troops and installations by air, up to then carried out by one pesky and elusive plane at a time? Would there be, following the relative inactivity that had lately prevailed along the battle-front, an all-out enemy attack on the ground, signifying the start of the third phase of what until five days

187

earlier could be called the spring offensive? Or, to cite one more of the many speculations that were circulated widely, would any of the thousands of Communist guerrillas still prowling behind our lines choose to mark the special day by doing something especially annoying? The big surprise proved, of course, to be Jakob Malik's provocative espousal of a cease-fire, which, rapidly disseminated by radio, telephone, and grapevine, was no less exciting an offering for having been delivered, as it was, twenty-four hours ahead of the anniversary.

General Van Fleet, whose formal statements have not always been notable for their clarity or pithiness, summed up his soldiers' reaction to the unanticipated development very neatly when he remarked, informally, "I'll be damned." As for the soldiers themselves, the ones I saw seemed to be indulging in little of the spontaneous rejoicing one might have expected would result from a statement like the Malik one. One grimy G.I. was told the news as he came in off a patrol, and asked if he planned to celebrate. "If I get some beer, I'll celebrate," he said. "I always find something to celebrate when I get beer." Doubtless the restraint with which the news was received was occasioned to some degree by the recipients' reluctance to build themselves up uncomfortably

188

high in the face of what could be a particularly dis-couraging letdown. (Not long before, in an Army hospital corridor, I had come across a sign that said, as if to remind all who saw it of the possible endlessness of the conflict, "Turn in your winter clothes. You may need them next winter. Who knows?") And there was also a lot of plain skepticism. "If the Commies really want a settlement along the Parallel," one soldier said on June 24th, "why didn't they make their bid a few weeks ago, when both sides were just about on it, instead of waiting till we'd pushed north of it again?" But despite this sort of talk, it was nonetheless briefly felt by some men up front that maybe the best birthday present of all, from their point of view—an end to hostilities—would, in swift response to the Malik speech, come their way on the twenty-fifth. This feeling, in turn, caused several combat commanders to take an ironically ungrateful view of the Soviet gesture. "I wish we could have kept the news from the troops," one officer told me. "Now that they think there's a good chance everything may be over in short order, it's inevitable that some of them will ease up. No-body wants to be the last man killed in a war. It doesn't rate the same kind of glory that the first man gets."

189

There were hardly any celebrations planned in advance by the Army for what might prove to be either the first or the only anniversary of the Korean War. I heard one group of men, on awakening in their tent near the front, greet the dawn of the twenty-fifth with a stirring rendition of a suitable song—"Happy birthday, dear police action, happy birthday to you!" On a more sombre note, a number of combat outfits held memorial ceremonies in recognition of the previous year's depletion of their ranks. Up in the 1st Cavalry Division sector, where I happened to be spending a few days, a fancy sign had been erected beside a road that cuts the Thirty-eighth Parallel at right angles, informing passersby that the war started there on June 25, 1950. But within a few yards of this marker, hours after the text of the Malik statement had reached the scene, soldiers were digging in both north and south of the line, in sweaty evidence of their determination not to cease anything until a cease-fire had got much further than the conversational stage.

As it happened, there were two celebrations in the 1st Cavalry area, one on the twenty-fourth and one on the twenty-fifth, but neither had anything to do with local history. June 25th was also the anniversary —the seventy-fifth—of the Battle of the Little Big

190

Horn, in which part of one of the division's regiments, the 7th Cavalry, went down with General Custer. The latterday bearers of the 7th's colors put up a sign commemorating that bygone June day—a somewhat bigger sign, as a matter of fact, than the one commemorating the troopers' contemporary, and considerably more successful, stand—and held a frolic in observance of the occasion. The day before, the battalion of Thailand troops attached to the 1st Cavalry had rousingly celebrated their nation's equivalent of the Fourth of July. A few men from each company in the battalion were temporarily excused from combat so they could attend the shindig, which was held more than twenty miles north of Malik's proposed check point. An American general in attendance, who knew about the day's principal news, said in an address to the Thai soldiers, perhaps meaningfully and perhaps simply because he was a general speaking to troops, "We have more combat ahead of us." The 1st Cavalry band also showed up for the affair and, after startling some spectators by playing "Onward, Christian Soldiers" as background music for an exhortation by the Thai commander to his men, most of whom are Buddhists, fraternally lent some of its instruments to Thai musicians, who proceeded to give out with spirited versions of "Good-

191

night Irene" and "Blue Night," which the King of Thailand composed for the Broadway revue "Michael Todd's Peep Show." Since the Chinese were only half a mile away, it was possible that some of them heard these tuneful carryings on and deduced that they represented a favorable reaction to Mr. Malik's peace feeler.

It is conceivable, as far as soldiers who were in Korea that day are concerned, that June 25, 1951, will ultimately be considered a memorable day only by those few individuals who have a personal reason for remembering it—among them, I should imagine, a certain American private and a certain British major. The private had been ordered, about the time Malik was talking, to escort four mules to a unit that, for some obscure purpose, had requisitioned them, and it was only in the last hours of the anniversary day, after a long and troubled search around the forward areas with his unco-operative companions, that he was able to complete his irksome mission. The major, a Royal Horse Guards officer who on June 25th the year before had been stationed in London, where he had had a command in the annual Trooping of the Color, on June 8th, will undoubtedly long regard the sweltering, enervating June 25th of 1951 as a particularly notable one, because he received on it a hot-water bottle

192

that he had plaintively requested from a friend in London the previous January. There were plenty of people in Korea on the day the hot-water bottle arrived who would have maintained that it might yet come in handy. Presumably this would have been the view of one G.I., who, on learning that a buddy of his, a baker, was to be rotated home on the twenty-fifth, made a remark that perhaps summarized the feeling in Korea as well as any other. When the baker said jokingly that as a parting remembrance to his chums he would leave behind a fresh birthday cake, with one candle on it, his friend said, not altogether jokingly, "Maybe you better add one to grow on while you're at it." If the second candle were to prove to be superfluous after all, an awful lot of birthday boys would have had their fondest wish come true.

14

On my return to the United States from Korea, I scanned with considerable interest the reports and laments being filed from there by my erstwhile colleagues. When I read a *New York Herald Tribune* story by Dave McConnell in which he described a nostalgic tour of the countryside he had just made in the company of two men he had toured it with six months earlier—Captain Hendrick Stone and Corporal Frederick Clifford, of the 25th Division—I was mildly afflicted with nostalgia myself, inasmuch as I, too, had bounced around Korea in a jeep with the two of them, they being the public-information officer of

194

the division and his driver, respectively. I also found McConnell's story quite enlightening, for, owing to the informality with which correspondents are privileged to associate with military personnel on almost every level, I had never known Captain Stone by any first name but Hank, and had assumed it was short for Henry. So it was Hendrick, was it! After finishing McConnell's story, in which Stone and Clifford were quoted as if they were just ordinary American soldiers who didn't spend, as they did, practically all their time with the press, I was not terribly surprised by a United Press dispatch I happened upon, a piece describing the reaction to Malik's cease-fire speech. The first American whose reaction was cited was, naturally, General Van Fleet. The second was Captain Harold Cheatham, of Birmingham, Alabama. This gave me pause, because Hal Cheatham, whom I had seen the day that story was written and who I recalled was then a first lieutenant, was a public-information officer at Eighth Army headquarters. He lived right with the press, and I couldn't help admiring the U.P. for having found a satisfactorily articulate soldier so close at hand, instead of, say, taking a long and dusty jeep ride toward the front in search of one.

The press in Korea could hardly be blamed in the

195

days immediately following the start of the Kaesong negotiations for picking up whatever scraps of information it could wherever it could, for I gathered that during the two weeks after I left it had been rather cooped up. Until the meetings at Kaesong began, there were almost never more than forty correspondents at the Eighth Army press billets, in Seoul. I read one day in July that facilities had been improvised there for housing two hundred of them. Many of the correspondents seemed to be staying, though, at a field camp set up in an orchard at Munsan, fourteen miles from Kaesong. During the initial sessions at Kaesong, to which, of course, the United Nations correspondents were not invited, they appeared to have diverted themselves at Munsan by thinking up original datelines to denote their involuntary halting place—with the conspicuous exception, that is, of the Associated Press men, whose stories filed from there were bluntly datelined "Munsan." The *New York Times* conceived "South of Kaesong," which sounded closer to the convention city than an outright pinpoint location would have. The *Herald Tribune* came up with "At Advance Camp of Cease-Fire Mission in Korea," which sounded as if the *Tribune* were at least three paddy fields closer to the key spot than the *Times*. The International News

196

Service favored "U.N. Truce Camp Near Kaesong," and the U.P. liked, depending on its mood, "U.N. Advanced Base Below Kaesong," "Advance U.N. Base Below Kaesong," or "U.N. Advance Camp Below Kaesong." Frank Bartholomew, a U.P. vice-president, who dashed to the Orient soon after Malik stopped talking and (at least according to U.P. dispatches) played a prominent role from then on in the jousting between the press and the military authorities, was partial to his own personal dateline: "On Imjin River South of Kaesong." I could think of no reason he couldn't compose his copy there if he chose to; I knew of a couple of fairly substantial, if temporary, bridges across the Imjin, on which he could doubtless find a spot to set his typewriter. Just the same, I should think he'd have been more comfortable if he'd gone ashore.

Bartholomew, as nearly as I could make out, was the highest-ranking newspaperman in the vicinity of Kaesong (I wondered how the U.P. underlings who had been in Korea for months felt about his pre-empting many of the by-lines they would have been getting if he hadn't showed up), and it was he who first formally complained to General Ridgway about the inadequacy of the provisions for covering the cease-fire negotiations and about the all-around inadequacy of Ridgway's public-information officers and censors. That a vice-president of the United Press should have been in the forefront of this particular battle surprised me a little, for not long before, while I was in Korea, a U.P. man had written a story in which he said that the correspondents there were of the unanimous opinion that the public-information and censorship setup was just dandy. In preparing the story, incidentally, he neglected to solicit the views of all his brother-correspondents, some of whom would have urged him to substitute some less sweeping word for "unanimous." One point of dissension between the press and the military at Munsan was the correspondents' conviction that the Communists would enjoy a propaganda advantage as the result of their having several photographers at the preliminary meetings at Kaesong and our having only a single Army corporal to take pictures. In explanation of how this disparity could work against the United Nations, the *World-Telegram & Sun* ran a story on July 9th that dwelt bitterly upon one shot that the corporal (and possibly the Communists, too) had made. It showed two American colonels riding in a Communist jeep while a Communist officer perched behind, looking down on them. The *World-Telegram* thought this picture might convey the notion that the colonels were prisoners of the man looming behind them. "The Communists, had they been asked, no doubt would have explained that the seats of honor were being given to the visitors and that the Red officer was riding on the rough rear edge of the jeep," the *Telegram* said, ignoring the fact that in jeep circles there is only one seat of honor, that alongside the driver, which is widely recognized not merely as the ranking one but the one easiest on the kidneys—a seat that in this instance was occupied by a Communist officer. "But pictures, unfortunately, will not give that impression to the rest of the world." Maybe not, but that particular picture gave no other impression to the *Daily Mirror*, an uncommonly alert journal when it comes to Communist tricks, which ran it with the unamplified caption "Envoys Ride to Parley in U.S. Style."

Besides, if the *World-Telegram* was really so concerned about how people were going to interpret photographs, it seemed odd that it hadn't objected to an A.P. Radiophoto published in New York on July 9th, which showed Governor Dewey and General Ridgway examining a document identified as Ridgway's reply to one of the Communist radio messages that preceded the negotiations. The inference could have been drawn from this shot that Ridgway had

199

submitted his message to Dewey for approval, and surely the *Telegram* ought to have been distraught about something that could have been interpreted by naïve and impressionable people as partisan political interference in grave affairs of state. The expenses of Dewey's jaunt were paid by *Collier's*, and I'd have bet it was a relief to the permanent *Collier's* representatives in Ridgway's territory—especially after watching Bartholomew move in on *his* boys—when the Governor, instead of covering the cease-fire sessions, stayed only briefly in Korea and then pushed along back to Japan and on to the less competitive territory of Formosa. The *World-Telegram* story about jeep protocol wasn't attributed to any source. It might have come in by way of the U.P., with which the paper is affiliated, or it might have been furnished by Jim Lucas, the Scripps-Howard man over there, who has an inimitable style, which was typified by the lead paragraph of one of his stories: "At least we were certain of one thing—the kid never knew what hit him." While I was in Korea, writing a piece on the typewriter I had been using almost daily for the better part of three months, I came across a Lucas story in which, to impress on his readers how bad the dust there can be, he broke all records for dust stories by stating that a typewriter exposed to it lasted only two days. Lucas, as it happened, had just lost a typewriter—it was apparently stolen—but he didn't mention this in the story. I could see what he was up to, though; he was covering himself with the home office in case the Scripps-Howard executive in charge of expense accounts should accuse him of irresponsibility.

Evidently, one of the most rousing battles that the correspondents in Korea had with the armed forces was precipitated by the military's misleading reference to Kaesong as an open city, though it contained a good deal of armed Communist soldiery, and by the military's subsequent attempt to prevent the press from reporting on this boner. The leader of the enraged fourth estate in this skirmish appeared to be Fred Sparks, of the Chicago *Daily News*—a singular reporter for several reasons, one being that he declines, in an era when it is decidedly inconvenient to cover wars merely by land and sea transport, to climb into an airplane unless he absolutely has to. (I feel a kinship with Sparks, for one day around the first of June, when we were both in Taegu, we were the only correspondents there who received any mail, and we received a lot—seventy-three letters for him, as I remember it, and twenty-two for me. Furthermore, we both got an exceptionally satisfying batch; his in-

201

cluded a five-hundred-dollar check from the Pulitzer Prize Committee, an award for a series of articles about Germany, and mine included a gift certificate from Brooks Brothers in the amount of eight dollars and twenty-four cents, entitling me to one yellow button-down shirt.) Sparks, it seemed, told a censor on General Ridgway's staff that he was going to describe Kaesong as a non-open city, whereupon the censor told him that such information would not be passed. Then Sparks, and a chorus of fellow-correspondents of undisclosed strength, announced they'd send it out anyway.

A United Press account of this contretemps in the *Mirror*, possibly cleared by another censor, had the censor involved in the dispute replying "tartly" to Sparks. The *Herald Tribune* ran the same story, but omitted the "tartly." The editors of the *Tribune* may have excised the adverb on the ground that the censors had been beaten over the head enough as it was. Whatever their reason, I suspected that the deletion was resented by Dave McConnell, one of the Far East's most gifted censor-baiters, who got in a few characteristic licks one day when, immediately following his "At Advance Camp of Cease-Fire Mission in Korea" dateline, he wrote, "United Nations heavy artillery rumbled in the background tonight

202

as I stood in a railroad car listening to military spokes-
men doing their best to provide no information on the
first day of cease-fire talks at Kaesong between U.N.
and Communist negotiators." Bert Andrews, the other
Tribune man then on the Tokyo-Korea beat, was
slightly more restrained. "Press arrangements for
American coverage of the preliminary and main
talks," he wrote three days before, "are going to be
unusual."

None of the papers said whether these arrangements would provide for the coverage of the
negotiations by Miss Betty Betz, a *very* unusual correspondent, who at home does a syndicated disserta-
tion on teen-age mores for King Features. She arrived
in Tokyo shortly before I left. As soon as I got back to
the States, I began searching the *New York Journal-
American* to see what sort of copy Miss Betz, herself a
bit beyond teen age, was filing from overseas, but I
was rewarded with only her conventional output,
which she probably produces well ahead of publica-
tion and, to cite part of a typical effort, goes like this:
"So you're trying to corner the market and get a ham-
merlock on the lad's affections? Before you race your
motor, remember that some gents are extremely
doll-shy. . . . Only those cornball Casanovas pour on
the drool talk anyway!" There would have been a

203

good piece for Miss Betz in the average age of the correspondents who covered the war. They were astonishingly young, if not necessarily doll-shy. For several months prior to the cease-fire talks, for instance, the oldest I.N.S. man in Korea was a creaking twenty-six. Not long before my departure for home, I was chatting with a correspondent, aged twenty-eight, who remarked that while staying at one division command post along with eight other correspondents, he had been flabbergasted to realize all at once that he was the oldest of the lot.

· Back at the beginning of the cease-fire discussions, General Ridgway advanced the argument that the negotiations themselves might be more important than the degree to which the press participated in them. Whether his modification of his initially restrictive attitude toward the correspondents and his abortive dispatch of twenty of them toward Kaesong, which brought the whole proceedings to one of their first standstills, proved that he should have held steadfast and not yielded to the anguished demands of the frustrated press, I still don't know. Knowing the difficulties a correspondent could experience in filing the most innocuous story from Korea, however, I could sympathize with the press in its exasperation. I found it harder to sympathize with the tendency of some journalists in this country to blame the military, and particularly the censors, for any old thing that seemed amiss. Take a waspish column by I. F. Stone in one issue of the New York *Compass*, under the heading "Ridgway Pulls a MacArthur—The Sour Note from Tokyo." Referring to a conference Ridgway had had with President Rhee in Pusan just after the Malik proposal, Stone wrote, "Washington was beginning to ask: 'Which side is Ridgway on? Rhee's or Truman's?' What was Ridgway's mission in Pusan? He was overheard saying to Rhee, 'Mr. President, I have been instructed to tell you . . .' At that point the censor's blue pencil went into action. What were the words deleted?" Stone's ringing question might have sounded a less sour note for me if there hadn't been, on the preceding page of that issue of the *Compass*, the A.P. news story from Pusan in which Ridgway's remark to Rhee was first revealed; in this the A.P. correspondent, Tom Bradshaw, stated, directly after the three dots, "The remainder of the remark was not heard." I had been in Korea when Ridgway's provocative remark was made, and I knew there was nothing sinister about its having been fragmentarily reported. What happened was that Ridgway and Rhee were walking away from Bradshaw as they struck up their conversation, and ambled out of earshot at that point in the General's sentence.

Considering the limitations that were imposed on the correspondents in Seoul and Munsan, there was astonishingly good coverage of the first talks at Kaesong. I have no idea how many attempts were made by people who hadn't yet seen it to describe the building at Kaesong in which the conferences were held, but some of the early stabs at it were valiant: "sumptuous private home" (*Times*), "simply decorated home" (A.P. in the *Compass*), "once-rich Korean home" (different A.P. man but same page, same paper), and so on. Then there was the perplexing business about the "W" with which the Communists marked the spot where they wanted our helicopters to land. The A.P. and U.P. agreed that it was red-and-white; the *Times* defiantly called it plain white. Nobody, in a corps of correspondents among whom the art of speculation had been perfected, came up with any plausible explanation of the "W." Just as historians may find this alphabetical teaser hard to figure out, they may be unable to decide what were the very first words uttered in Kaesong by the very first American to utter any there—Colonel Andrew J. Kinney. The *Times*, which puts out a rag-paper edition and is thus most likely to be consulted by scholars, had him saying, "Let's get down to business," but nearly all the other accounts of his terse conversational gambit went along with the A.P., which quoted him as reporting, "I said, 'Let's sit down to business.' That's exactly what I said."

A record of nearly every morsel of food consumed —or, for that matter, not consumed—by our negotiators was faithfully set down for posterity. The *Times*, fittingly, recorded the most. George Barrett, a many-faceted *Times* man who carried a copy of Jung's *Psychology of the Unconscious* around with him and was given to characterizing his own stories as "cute," revealed that General Van Fleet's mess sergeant, in anticipation of our emissaries' treks to Kaesong, had assembled, on a truck, for their use five hundred pounds of steak, a hundred and eighty of ham, a hundred of turkey, sixty of pork, and a side of veal, weight unspecified. The mess sergeant, while he was at it, threw in twenty pounds of rice, some soy sauce, and "a thick bundle" of chopsticks. (The purpose of these last was not made clear; they may have been for any Communists who felt like breaking bread with our delegates or they may have been for the Asian members of our negotiating parties.) But two days later Barrett was saying, a trifle anticlimactically, that the first meal eaten in Kaesong by the first United Nations representatives to get there consisted of cold roast beef and cold turkey sandwiches. He didn't say what had happened to the mess sergeant's groaning truck. Most of the other correspondents concentrated on the food and liquor—candy, vodka, beer, *sake*, and so forth—that the Communists in Kaesong offered our people. It was quite generally agreed that the United Nations delegates spurned these refreshments, politely but frostily. The *Daily Worker*, however, reported that one helicopter pilot had sampled some Communist beer and pronounced it "not bad."

Barrett specialized not only in food but also in headgear. On June 25th, the day after all the hubbub started, he wrote (I was right next to him but had no idea what was on his mind or in his typewriter) that, as a result of the mounting speculation about an imminent end to hostilities, there was a spirited demand among the American soldiers for Korean money, so they could go to the markets and buy, as souvenirs, some of the tall black horsehair hats that venerable Korean men wear outdoors. (I hated to think what would happen if this story was an accurate reflection of the soldiers' ambitions, for I had just brought one hat home, and it was a frightful task; the fragility of the hat is such that it has to be carried by hand.) A week later, evidently having concluded that the soldiers were not quite so optimistic after all, Barrett reported, "They want to see something signed, sealed, and delivered before they will throw their fatigue caps into the air." He failed to take into account the notorious persuasiveness of news photographers, for only six days after that—considerably before anything had been signed, sealed, and delivered—the *New York Post* had been able to publish a photograph of half a dozen soldiers in Korea with fatigue caps indisputably in the air above their up-stretched arms.

Photographers are apt to be looked down on by those who deal solely in words, and the cameramen in Korea must have got a big bang out of the fact that five of their caste were chosen by the Army as the first civilian correspondents to enter Kaesong—this on the second day Admiral Joy and his crew went there— and were permitted not only to take pictures but to write a collective story for the theoretically more literate correspondents. (Bartholomew, in his account of this partial victory over the forces of repression, mentioned the name of only one of the chosen five— Jim Healy, of Acme, the U.P.'s picture agency; I.N.S. gallantly gave the entire roster.) The photographers were authorized to make the trip by Brigadier General Frank A. Allen, Jr., who had just become Ridg-way's chief press-relations man and, having filled a similar role for General Eisenhower in 1945, seemed well on his way to becoming a man who helped, or hindered, the press in its coverage of two wars' ends. Allen's justification for letting the lucky quintet go to Kaesong was that the Communists had agreed to the admittance there of five "Army photographers" from each side; the General pointed out that since all correspondents are accredited to the Army, the photographers could be said to be Army personnel. Apparently, this logic was accepted without protest by the entire press corps. I'd have been happier if somebody had registered a mild complaint, for it would seem that General Allen, no matter how he might think he had assisted the press by his decision, had got away with establishing a dangerous principle; namely, that there's no difference worth quibbling over between a civilian correspondent and a soldier. (A lot of members of the armed forces did excellent work as combat correspondents, but they were always subject not only to censorship but to routine military supervision, and were accordingly somewhat restricted in their endeavors.) At that, the five photographers weren't able to enjoy exclusively their temporary designation as Army cameramen. An A.P.

210

dispatch from Munsan, filed coincidentally with the pooled story of the five photographers, said that there was a sixth United Nations photographer in Kaesong the same day—a Far Eastern Command photographic officer, equipped with one of those Polaroid Land cameras that can almost instantaneously produce prints. He, however, brought only five pictures back to Munsan with him; he took a good many more than that, but it seemed that the Communist subjects of his pictures were fascinated with the rapid developing and printing of which his camera is capable, and he blithely presented them with all but the five shots. Maybe it's just as well that we're not entirely dependent for pictures, or news, on members of the armed forces.